Team
Workout

A Trainer's Sourcebook of
50 Team-Building
Games and Activities

Glenn Parker
Richard Kropp

AMACOM
American Management Association
New York • Atlanta • Boston • Chicago • Kansas City • San Francisco • Washington, D.C.
Brussels • Mexico City • Tokyo • Toronto

Special discounts on bulk quantities of AMACOM books are available to corporations, professional associations, and other organizations. For details, contact Special Sales Department, AMACOM, a division of American Management Association, 1601 Broadway, New York, NY 10019.
Tel.: 212-903-8316. Fax: 212-903-8083.
Web site: www.amacombooks.org

Library of Congress Cataloging-in-Publication Data

Parker, Glenn M., 1938–
   Team workout: a trainer's sourcebook of 50 team-building games and activities / Glenn Parker, Richard Kropp.
      p.   cm.
   Includes index.
   ISBN 0-8144-7120-X (pbk.)
   1. Teams in the workplace—Problems, exercises, etc.   2. Group games.   3. Group relations training.   I. Kropp, Richard P.   II. Title.

HD66.P348   2001
658.4' 02—dc21

                                                      2001018924

Printing number

10 9 8 7 6 5 4 3 2 1

Contents

Acknowledgments   v

Part 1: Introduction   1

What Is a Team?   4
Types of Teams   4
Team Building and Team Training   6
How to Use the Activities, Assessments, Case Studies, and Other
    Experiential Learning Methods   6

Part 2: Activities   9

1. Bringing Up the Boss   11
2. Building Trust among Team Players: Trust Is All We Have to Lose   13
3. Characteristics of an Effective Work Team: An Assessment Activity   17
4. Choice Role: A Role-Clarification Activity   25
5. Communicating about Conflict: Learning Ways to Resolve Conflict   31
6. Creating a Team Logo   37
7. Creating a Team Mission: A Team-Development Activity   39
8. Customer Delight: A Data-Collection Tool   47
9. Drawings: Improving Collaboration among Teams   53
10. E-Handles: A Closing Activity for a Mature Team   55
11. Forming New Teams: A Get-Acquainted and Introductory Activity   59
12. Freeze Frame: Dealing with Problem Behaviors in Teams   73
13. Got Culture? A Team-Assessment Tool   75
14. Get SMART: Goal-Setting Skill Development   85
15. How Do You Like to Receive Recognition? A Self-Assessment   93
16. How's Your Team's Vision? A Team-Development Activity   101
17. Improving Team Meetings   109
18. It's a Puzzlement: A Get-Acquainted Icebreaker   113
19. Meeting Monsters: Dealing with Problem People on Teams   121

iv   **Contents**

20. My Team and Me: Increasing Team Members' Identification with the
    Team   127
21. Personal Ads: A Large-Group Icebreaker   133
22. Project Rescue   143
23. Really . . . but I Thought   149
24. Refreshing the Team: Taking Stock of Where We Have Been and
    What We Need to Do to Move Ahead   151
25. R E S P E C T: An Assessment Instrument   155
26. Rhyme Time: A Game That Teaches Team Concepts   167
27. Roadblocks: A Constraint Activity   179
28. Selecting a Problem Solution   189
29. Separate Tables: Resolving Intergroup Conflict   197
30. Skills for Sale: An Assessment Simulation   201
31. SOS: An OD Intervention   203
32. Team-Building Interview Guide   209
33. Team Conflict Mode   213
34. Team Development: A Grid Perspective   219
35. Teams That Change: Building a Team Plan for Change   225
36. Tell-a-Story Teaming: An Exercise in Creativity and Productivity   227
37. The Car Case: Learning How to Define a Problem   231
38. The Case of the Free-Falling Team: Developing High-Performing
    Team Players   235
39. The Collaborative: Creating the Conditions for the Collaborative
    Team   239
40. The Effective Team Member: A Consensus-Building Group-on-
    Group Activity   243
41. The Product Development Team: A Simulation   253
42. The Quality Case: An Ethical Dilemma   261
43. The Way We Are, and Want to Be: A Visioning
    Activity for an Intact Team   267
44. TMS: A Process for Role Clarification   273
45. Tricky Tales: A Cross-Team-Building Approach   279
46. Tough Jobs: A Consensus-Building Activity   295
47. Virtual Brainstorming: Problem-Solving for a Geographically
    Dispersed Team   305
48. Virtual Consensus: Participative Decision-Making without a Meeting 309
49. Wisdom: An Intergroup Team Game   311
50. Yea, Team! A Large-Group Icebreaker   325

Team Workout Resources   333

Topical Index of Activities   335

Index   341

About the Authors   345

Acknowledgments

We would like to thank Kristen Ciolkosz for her help in editing and compiling the activities. Her diligence and attention to detail are admirable.

We would also like to acknowledge our friend, collaborator, and supporter, Chris Hunter of HRD Press, who believes in our work and in us. His contribution is immeasurable.

Glenn Parker
Skillman, New Jersey
June 2000

Dick Kropp
Scituate, Massachusetts
June 2000

Part 1

Introduction

Introduction

Team Workout is a natural extension of our best-selling book, *50 Activities for Team Building*, volume 1, published by HRD Press in 1992. Selected by *Human Resource Executive* magazine as one of the Top Ten Training Tools of 1992, *50 Activities for Team Building* went on to become one of HRD Press's most successful publications, and still enjoys wide popularity.

In the interim, the business world changed dramatically, as did our knowledge of teams in the workplace. New demands on organizations and new challenges for facilitators, team-building consultants, and managers have combined to create a need for new activities and extensive revisions of classic exercises that address the current reality.

Team Workout answers the need for both. It is a unique combination of new activities that focus on such current team issues as virtual teams, trust building, change management, customer satisfaction, and recognition and respect as well as refreshed versions of classic assessment tools and icebreakers that address issues surrounding ethics, consensus building, meetings management, and problem-solving. All of the exercises have been tested and used many times with our clients.

We have created this book for a variety of audiences:

1. **Team-Building Facilitators**. Many of the exercises are designed for use with intact teams that have either been diagnosed with a variety of problems or that must address key issues such as internal conflict, mission, or respect.
2. **Trainers**. A large number of the activities have been developed for use in training sessions designed to address team needs in such areas as problem-solving, ethics, decision-making, team meetings, and quality.
3. **Managers and Coaches**. Team coaches and managers of team-based organizations will find a number of organizational and team-assessment

instruments, visioning exercises, and intergroup activities that can be used effectively organizationwide or with specific teams.

4. **Meeting Planners**. Many large-group activities included in this new book are suitable for corporate meetings and organizational conferences. Icebreakers, group exercises, and fun activities engage people and build energy, as well as teach important points.

What Is a Team?

A group of people does not necessarily make a team. A team can be defined as a group of individuals with a high degree of interdependence, focused on the achievement of some goal or task. The group agrees on the goal and knows that the way to achieve that goal is to work together.

Some groups have a common goal but do not work together to achieve it, while other groups work well together even without a common goal. The purpose of this collection of activities is to help those team leaders, team-building specialists, trainers, as well as those interested in creating collaborative work teams, bring two or more individuals into harmony and make them effective.

Many skills are needed to be truly effective as a team leader or team developer. This manual provides a collection of activities that can be used with intact work teams or training groups who will go back to their work environment and build effective teams.

The philosophy that underlies all of the activities in this manual revolves around three key ideas:

1. Each team has a common purpose, mission, or goal.
2. The members are interdependent; they need each other to achieve their purpose.
3. They agree that they must work together effectively to reach their goal.

Teams have become important structures in today's organizations. Since the mid-twentieth century, the "team" form of organization has continued to evolve, from informal working groups to self-directed virtual communities where members rarely meet face-to-face. As traditional forms of organization are replaced by new, yet-to-be-defined structures, the need to create interdependent units has become greater. This need is compounded by the globalization of business and technology, and a changing workforce composed of new values, new needs, and new desires.

Types of Teams

Teams come in many shapes and sizes. The basic work team is usually a manager and his or her direct reports. Teams can also be ad hoc groups, such as task forces or committees, that come together for a specific purpose and a limited time period. One recent phenomenon, the cross-functional team, brings together experts from a variety of disciplines and departments to develop new products or systems or achieve other results.

We can distinguish teams by three dimensions:

1. **Purpose**. It could be product development, quality, marketing, systems, etc.
2. **Duration**. It is either permanent or ad hoc.
3. **Membership**. It could be functional or cross-functional.

We can divide teams up into five main types:

1. **Natural Work Groups.** Groups composed of people who work together every day.
2. **Business Team.** Groups of people who come together for a specific task or project.
3. **Management Team.** Groups of people, usually peer managers, who come together to coordinate the actions of an entire organization.
4. **Problem-Solving Team.** Groups of people who come together for a specific period of time to analyze a given situation and make recommendations for working alternatives.
5. **New Product/Service Teams.** Groups of people who come together, perhaps cross-functionally, to design or redesign a product or service.

The most challenging teams are the cross-functional, ad hoc teams. Although the payoff is potentially great, the purpose of the team is unclear, and the task of forging an effective team is complicated by the different styles that the people from various disciplines bring to the table. The temporary nature of the relationship often decreases the motivation to work hard on building an effective team, adding to the challenge.

Activities, assessments, case studies, games, and other experiential learning methods are structured processes that challenge participants to explore their thoughts, feelings, attitudes, and knowledge and to share the products of this exploration with their colleagues. The products of these explorations are actions that offer new ways and means to help the team achieve their goals.

Team Workout provides facilitators, trainers, leaders, and managers with a wide variety of tools to increase team effectiveness and upgrade skills and knowledge within today's challenging organizational environment. A topical index helps you select the activity that best addresses your needs.

Team Building and Team Training

Team building is a data-based intervention that assesses the strengths and improvement opportunities of a work team and then prepares and implements plans to increase the effectiveness of the team. Team building also increases the ability of the team to diagnose and solve its own problems.

The term *team building* is often used to describe what we would call "training in team effectiveness." Training focuses on increasing the effectiveness of individuals by providing them with skills and knowledge to improve their job performance. Team-effectiveness training is, therefore, a program that increases the ability of people to function as members or leaders of a team.

Participants in a workshop on teamwork generally come from a variety of teams. In some instances, entire teams come to a workshop and benefit from learning together. In these cases, training can approximate team building if the team assesses its effectiveness and uses the learning from the workshop to improve its performance.

Team-effectiveness training provides participants with skills and knowledge to increase their personal effectiveness and, ultimately, the effectiveness of their teams. The training will include topics such as problem-solving, decision-making, communications, goal-setting, meeting management, conflict resolution, the use of research tools and presentation skills, and factors for team success.

In this sourcebook, we have included activities that can be used in both team building and team training. As appropriate, we distinguish between those activities that are better used in training and those that are more effective for team-building purposes.

How to Use the Activities, Assessments, Case Studies, and Other Experiential Learning Methods

Thiagarajan and Parker in their book *Teamwork and Teamplay*[1] offer several important insights about how to use activities, assessments, case studies, and experiential learning methods. We have adapted them for this manual.

Before Conducting the Activity

1. Select the most appropriate activity. This manual provides a matrix of activities and topic areas to help you select the best activity for your specific application.
2. Review the activity with your client or others to make sure that the need and the activity are a good match.

3. Conduct a practice session. Review the entire activity and make sure you have mastered the process.
4. Estimate the number of participants, and make certain that you have the proper materials and supplies.
5. Specify the overall goals and objectives for the workshop or intervention and how they relate to larger organizational goals.
6. Plan your briefing procedure. Prepare a list of discussion questions so that participants can reflect on their performance, gain useful insights, and share information with one another.
7. Anticipate the need to recover. A disaster might occur, so plan for some what-if questions.

During the Activity

1. Get into the activity as quickly as possible. Keep your opening comments limited and focused on the action.
2. Present the activity and its steps. Assign any roles that might be required, and distribute the necessary activity materials.
3. Ask for any questions and let the participants know that there might be some moments of confusion at the start of an activity, but the purpose will soon become clear.
4. Don't interfere with the group once the activity has begun. Let it take its course.
5. Bring the activity to a defined conclusion at the end of the assigned time period or when the goal is achieved.

After the Activity

1. Conduct a debriefing discussion. Each of the activities in this volume has a set of debriefing questions that you might use for your interventions. These are just guides; add or take out material as you wish.
2. Ask the participants to report on what they learned from the activity. Also ask them for their action plans based on the newly learned procedures and ideas.
3. Invite the participants to ask you questions about the activity and the learning outcomes.

Notes

1. S. Thiagarajan and G. Parker, *Teamwork and Teamplay: Games and Activities for Building and Training Teams.* San Francisco: Jossey-Bass/Pfeiffer, 1999.

Part 2

Activities

Activity 1

Bringing Up the Boss

Purpose

1. To help an intact work team quickly become familiar with a new team leader
2. To help a new team leader lay a foundation for team effectiveness
3. To demonstrate the importance of open communication

Group Size

A new or intact team of up to fifteen members, with a new leader

Time

90 minutes

Physical Setting

A room large enough for the group to work comfortably, with chairs arranged in a circle or with a table and chairs arranged in seminar style

Materials

Easel, flipchart pad, markers, and masking tape or push pins

Process

1. New team leaders should begin by telling the team they want to get to know members quickly and open lines of communication. The team leader explains the agenda, introduces the facilitator, and leaves the meeting.
2. The facilitator gives a brief talk about the assimilation curve of new team leaders and the need for open communication.
3. Participants are asked to pose questions to the new leader, such as:
   - What are your measures of success?
   - How do you like to work?
   - What turns you on or turns you off?

   The facilitator writes each question on the flipchart until all are listed.
4. The facilitator reviews and clarifies the list of questions.
5. The new team leader returns to the meeting and, guided by the facilitator, answers each question.
6. When all are answered, the leader gets to question the group.
7. The team leader then agrees to hold ongoing sessions to keep communication lines open. Meeting frequency, duration, and location are decided.
8. The facilitator summarizes the meeting.

Debriefing

1. To the manager or leader:
   - How did you feel about this activity?
   - Did it meet your expectations? Why? Why not?
   - Did you answer all of the participants' questions? Why or why not?
   - Were you surprised by any of the questions?
   - What question did the team not ask that you expected it to ask?
   - How will you behave now, given this activity?

2. To the team members:
   - How did you feel about this activity?
   - Did it meet your expectations? Why or why not?
   - Were all the questions answered?
   - What would you like to see done differently?
   - What will you do with this new information about your team leader?

Variations

1. The team leader acts as facilitator.
2. Members can be asked to prepare their questions in advance of the meeting.
3. Additional questions can be asked by members after the team leader finishes asking his or her own questions (Step 6).

Activity 2

Building Trust among Team Players

Trust Is All We Have to Lose

Purpose

1. To develop problem-solving skills in a team
2. To develop interdependence and trust within a team

Group Size

Four is ideal; no more than five. Form as many teams as required.

Time

30 to 45 minutes

Physical Setting

A room large enough for the group to work comfortably.

Materials

1. One package each of red, white, and blue clay
2. Four or five blindfolds
3. A flat working surface, such as a desk or table

Process

1. Participants are asked to choose a team leader. The team leader blindfolds the remaining three participants. Instruct each team leader to do the following:
   a) Distribute one color clay to each of the three participants.
   b) The facilitator tells the team that they will make the American flag with the clay.
   c) Tell the person with the red clay to make the red stripes, the person with the white clay to make the stars and the white stripes (if five participants, divide this task), and the person with the blue clay to make the field for the stars.
   d) Tell the team leader to oversee the team's work and offer whatever verbal (no physical) assistance is necessary for members to make these individual parts of the flag. Allow 15 minutes to complete this task.
2. After individual pieces are made, blindfolds are removed. The team leader is now blindfolded. With verbal (no physical) directions from the team, the leader takes the red, white, and blue parts and assembles the flag. Allow about 8 to 10 minutes.
3. After the flag is completed, the team leader's blindfold is removed. General discussion follows, with members discussing: interaction, communication effectiveness, degree of encouragement and support, what worked well and what didn't, and ways the process might have been improved.
4. Conclude the activity by reviewing the concept of trust, using the lecture on trust provided. Then review the actions the team wishes to take, and agree on the next steps.

Debriefing

- What significant things did you learn about yourself from this exercise?
- What insights can you take away from the exercise that will help improve your team's effectiveness?
- What insights did you gain about the concept of trust?

Lecture Notes: **TRUST**

Trust refers to the willingness and the ability to rely on others to fulfill certain roles. Trust revolves around the issues of expectation, predictability of behaviors, and safety. There are a variety of ways in which the nature and characteristics of collaborative structures interact to make trust possible. It does not arise from naiveté or unrestrained optimism, but rather is a product of the forces at work to achieve success within collaborative structures.

In any situation where we interact with others to accomplish a task, we use *expectations* about another person's input to guide our actions. Whether we are manufacturing complex machinery, providing expert services, or planning a party, our expectations designate which types of behaviors and approaches we will see from specific people. Knowing how situations will be handled guides our own behavior and planning. We know who makes delicious desserts, who is good with crafts and decorations, and who can plan meals for large groups. And, as a result, we are inclined to ask these people to deal with situations that we feel are suited to the unique talents that they can bring to the party. We also know other characteristics, such as who is committed and whose feet will drag. The extent to which we believe that our expectations are accurate determines the amount of time and attention we devote to oversight, follow-up, and contingency plans. Based on some combination of these expectations, we choose which actions to take.

Trust also refers to the certainty people exhibit about others—the predictability of others' behavior. *Predictability,* while it is interwoven with expectations, is more concretely focused on the goals and behaviors we know others will use. We discuss this on a regular basis using terms like *acting in good faith* and *being reliable.* While expectations will tell us that a particular manager is fair, predictability will tell us how that is likely to be exhibited.

Being able to make such predictions allows us to more productively interact with others in two ways. First, we can concentrate on the task at hand without second-guessing or becoming overly bogged down in side issues. Secondly, predictability reduces misunderstanding and second-guessing, which can leave coworkers striving at cross purposes when they believe they are working together. Collaborative structures foster a predictability among members with regard to the process of interacting to solve problems and achieve success.

The third aspect of trust, *safety,* arises from specific expectations and predictions that are common to collaborative structures. Safety is an issue about the environment of achievement and problem-solving. Risk, in this sense, does not refer to implementing alternatives, but to recognizing them. The higher the risk of exploring alternative routes, the less exploration there will be. Thus, risky environments lead us to rely on habitual solutions without acknowledging alternatives. Risk increases when members of a group fear personal attack, censure, or evaluation based on criteria other than the merit of their ideas. The group thereby stifles itself; it sees no other way to do business except the way it has always been done.

The *collaborative* paradigm, by contrast, creates a safe working environment. The interaction of collaborative characteristics promotes the expectation that people will want to hear different ideas and viewpoints. Collaboration leads to the prediction that members will evaluate ideas on their merits, rather than on who proposed them or how "normal" the idea first sounds. People feel safe discussing ideas and alternatives, even those that apply "outside" their area of expertise. So, through trust, the group increases its opportunities to succeed and achieve.

Trust appears at two mutually reinforcing levels: Firstly, collaborative structures foster the development of expectations and predictions focused on issues critical to the group's success. There is increased safety in this approach, as we become more certain that others are capable of and committed to accomplishing their particular tasks. Secondly, collaborative structures emphasize "succeeding together" over succeeding or failing alone. This promotes discussion and the sharing of solutions to problems without fear of recrimination. So, it is more likely that all tasks will be completed successfully. Encouraging and making it safe for members to share ideas reinforces our faith in expectations and predictions.

Thus, trust appears as a willingness of members to rely on each other to fulfill specific roles, as well as the ability to rely on members accomplishing the tasks associated with those roles.

Activity 3

Characteristics of an Effective Work Team

An Assessment Activity

Purpose

1. To assess the effectiveness of a team
2. To plan for the improvement of a team

Group Size

Works best with an intact team of no more than twenty people

Time

2 hours, plus prework

Physical Setting

Chairs arranged in a circle, or tables and chairs arranged in a U-shape

---

Materials

1. A copy of *Characteristics of an Effective Work Team* for each person
2. A copy of *Interpreting Your Results* for each person
3. A copy of the *Action Planning Guide* for each person

Process

1. The survey should be completed by each person prior to the meeting. The facilitator should summarize the results and prepare a report for the team.
2. At the meeting, present the summary and ask the team to identify key strengths and improvement opportunities. Strengths are high in description and importance; improvement opportunities are low in description and high in importance. Distribute the handout *Interpreting Your Results.*
3. Isolate up to three key areas the team would like to address. If the team is small, the whole team can develop action plans for each area. With a large team, form subteams and ask each team to work on one of the areas.
4. Ask subgroups to present their action plans. Follow up with a discussion and plans for implementation.
5. The team should plan to periodically review their plans to monitor progress.
6. Debrief the session.

Debriefing

- How do you feel about this activity?
- What did you learn about the effectiveness of this team?
- Were there any surprises in the results?
- To what extent do you think people were honest in their assessment of the team?
- How confident are you that the team will follow through on the action plans?
- What other areas, not covered by the survey, does the team need to address?
- What things can you personally do to increase the effectiveness of the team?

Variations

1. Complete the survey in class and summarize the results on the flipchart.
2. Tailor the survey to reflect current issues on the team.
3. Interview team members instead of using a survey. See Activity 32: Team-Building Interview Guide.

Worksheet

Characteristics of an Effective Work Team

Please circle the number that indicates the degree to which you feel the following characteristics are descriptive of your team.

Circle the number that indicates the degree to which you feel each characteristic is important to the functioning of the team.

CHARACTERISTICS	DESCRIPTION NEVER / SELDOM / SOMETIMES / USUALLY / ALWAYS	IMPORTANCE UNIMPORTANT / SOMEWHAT IMPORTANT / IMPORTANT / VERY IMPORTANT / CRITICAL
1. **Clear Task.** The task or objective of the group is well understood and accepted by the group.	1 2 3 4 5	1 2 3 4 5
2. **Informality.** The atmosphere tends to be informal, comfortable, and relaxed. There are no obvious tensions or signs of boredom.	1 2 3 4 5	1 2 3 4 5
3. **Participation**. There is a lot of discussion in which virtually everyone participates, but it remains pertinent to the task of the group.	1 2 3 4 5	1 2 3 4 5
4. **Listening**. The members listen to each other. Every idea is given a hearing.	1 2 3 4 5	1 2 3 4 5

(continues)

(continued)

CHARACTERISTICS	DESCRIPTION					IMPORTANCE				
	NEVER	SELDOM	SOMETIMES	USUALLY	ALWAYS	UNIMPORTANT	SOMEWHAT IMPORTANT	IMPORTANT	VERY IMPORTANT	CRITICAL
5. **Disagreement**. There is disagreement, but the team is comfortable with it. There are no signs of avoiding conflict to keep everything sweet and light.	1	2	3	4	5	1	2	3	4	5
6. **Consensus**. Most decisions are reached by consensus. Formal voting is kept to a minimum.	1	2	3	4	5	1	2	3	4	5
7. **Open Communications**. Team members feel free to express their feelings on the task as well as the group's operation. There is very little hedging and there are few hidden agendas.	1	2	3	4	5	1	2	3	4	5
8. **Clear Assignment**. When action is taken, clear assignments are made and accepted.	1	2	3	4	5	1	2	3	4	5
9. **Shared Leadership**. While the team has a formal leader, leadership functions do shift from time to time, depending on the circumstances, the needs of the group, and the skills of the members.	1	2	3	4	5	1	2	3	4	5
10. **Self-Assessment**. Periodically, the team stops to examine how well it is functioning and what might be interfering with its effectiveness.	1	2	3	4	5	1	2	3	4	5

Worksheet *Interpreting Your Results*

1. **Strength = High importance and high description.** This characteristic is important to your success, and you use it well. You need to continue exhibiting this characteristic.

   High = A mean (average) of 3.5 or higher.

   Please list all of your strengths here:

   _____

   _____

   _____

   _____

   _____

2. **Improvement opportunity = High importance and low description.** This characteristic is important to your success, but you don't use it well. You need to improve.

   Low = A mean (average) of 3.4 or lower.

   Please list all of your improvement opportunities here:

   _____

   _____

   _____

   _____

   _____

Action Planning Guide

Directions: Select one of the improvement areas. Use this guide to develop an action plan for increasing the effectiveness of your team in this area.

1. **Problem statement**. Write a clear, one-sentence description of the problem.

   _____

   _____

   _____

2. **Problem analysis.** List the key causes of the problem.

   _____

   _____

   _____

3. **Alternative solutions**. Develop a list of potential solutions to the problem.

   _____

   _____

   _____

4. **Recommendations**. Provide a brief description of your proposed solution.

   _____

   _____

   _____

5. **Action plan**. List the steps you will follow to implement the solution.

   _____

   _____

   _____

Activity 4

Choice Role

A Role-Clarification Activity

Purpose

1. To help team members identify their roles
2. To clarify perceptions about the roles of team members
3. To generate feedback about each team member's role
4. To provide each team member with the opportunity to assume different roles on the team

---

Group Size

Designed primarily for an intact team of less than ten members. However, the activity is applicable to a team-training workshop where participants learn about team roles and gain insight into the role they typically play on a team.

Time

45 minutes

Physical Setting

Chairs set around a rectangular table or a set of tables, facing the overhead projector and screen

Materials

1. A copy of *Choice Role?* for each person
2. A transparency of the handout *Choice Roles*
3. An overhead projector, screen, acetates, and acetate markers

Process

1. Explain that the purpose of the activity is to gain clarity on the roles individuals play on teams and to increase team effectiveness by making sure all the key roles are filled.
2. Distribute the handout. Put up the overhead or take a few minutes to make comments and take questions clarifying the various roles described on the handout.
3. Ask participants to identify their primary role on the team. Indicate that you will also be asking for the reasons why the particular role was selected. Allow a few minutes of private time for this task.
4. Ask participants to present their answers. Make sure everyone presents. Facilitate discussion and feedback from teammates after each presentation. Ask others how their perceptions match with those of the individual presenting the answer. You can also ask team members to reveal their second choice.
5. Then ask participants to select roles they want to play in the future. Allow a few minutes for each person to make a selection. And once again, indicate that you will be asking the reasons for selecting a particular role.
6. Ask each person to present a future role. Facilitate discussion and feedback from teammates after each presentation.
7. Debrief the activity, using some or all of the questions provided.

Debriefing

- What did you learn about your teammates from this activity?
- What did you learn about yourself from this activity?
- In what ways was it helpful to get the feedback from your teammates on your selection? If your teammates' selection for you differed from yours, how does this help you? What did you (or can you) learn from this?
- Were there any surprises?
- How will this activity help the team become successful?

- Are there any key team roles missing on your team? What can you do to compensate for that role?
- What will (or should) the team do differently as a result of this activity?

Variations

1. Add a game element to the activity. After Step 3, ask team members to guess which role their teammates selected for themselves. They should write their list of guesses on a separate sheet of paper. After Step 4, ask participants to score their answers and reveal how many and which ones they guessed correctly. Give the person with the most correct answers the "Insight Award." Some additional facilitation opportunities might emerge at this point.

2. Change Step 5 to ask each team member to select a future role for the other teammates. Then, go around the team and ask each person to indicate which role they selected for a particular person. Once again, some additional facilitation opportunities might emerge from this activity.

3. Another game possibility is to give the "Openness Award" to the person whose selected role in Step 3 was correctly guessed by the most teammates.

Worksheet   *Choice Role?*

GATEKEEPER

STANDARD-SETTER

TASK MASTER

HISTORIAN

DEVIL'S ADVOCATE

INNOVATOR/CREATOR

FACILITATOR

PRIEST/RABBI

EXPERT

PARTY – PLANNER

INFORMATION-PROVIDER

VISIONARY

LISTENER

JOKESTER (TENSION RELIEVER?)

SUPPORTER

RISK-TAKER

CONSENSUS-BUILDER

PROCESS OBSERVER

Activity 5

Communicating about Conflict

Learning Ways to Resolve Conflict

Purpose

1. To share approaches to dealing with conflict in a team setting
2. To learn alternative approaches to dealing with conflict

Group Size

Four to twelve people is preferred. This exercise is most appropriate for team building, but it can be adapted for use in team-training workshops. In a workshop, a larger group can be divided into several subgroups for the purpose of this activity.

Time

1 to 2 hours

Physical Setting

For team building, arrange chairs in a circle. For training, arrange several groups of chairs in a circle, or use round tables and chairs.

Materials

1. A copy of *Communicating about Conflict* for each person.
2. Lecture notes, *Styles of Conflict Resolution,* for the facilitator. You can also use this as a handout.

Process

1. Explain the purpose of the exercise. Distribute the handout.
2. Ask for a volunteer to begin with the first question. Follow the directions on the handout.
3. The facilitator should probe for clarification, elaboration, and for appropriate interventions.
4. Summarize key points about conflict and what changes in the team are necessary in order to facilitate effective conflict resolution.
5. Debrief the exercise with the questions provided.
6. Conclude the session with a brief lecture or discussion on conflict styles and their advantages and disadvantages.

Debriefing

- How would you define conflict, now that you have completed this activity?
- Is it the same or different than before?
- What actions will you now take to make sure that conflict is positively addressed?
- How would you like your teammates to handle conflict?
- How would you describe the way your team handles conflict?
- How effective is the way your team handles conflict?

Variations

1. Change the questions and statements to more closely fit the issues on your team.
2. The facilitator or team members can demonstrate how persons with different conflict styles are likely to react to the various questions and comments.
3. The session can conclude with a discussion on how to handle conflict differently in the future. Make sure everyone participates.
4. For an exercise focusing on how a team deals with conflict, see Activity 33: Team Conflict Mode.

Communicating about Conflict

Instructions: The list of open-ended statements below are designed to stimulate group discussion. You are not limited to the ones on this list. The following ground rules apply:

- Take turns initiating the discussion by completing a statement or asking someone else on the team to complete a statement.
- You must be willing to complete any statement that you ask someone else to complete.
- Any member can decline to complete a statement that someone else initiates.
- All discussion remains confidential.

Statements can be taken in any order:

1. Conflict is . . .
2. The time I felt best about dealing with conflict was . . .
3. When things are not going well, I tend to . . .
4. I sometimes avoid unpleasant situations by . . .
5. When someone disagrees with me about something important, I usually . . .
6. When someone challenges me in front of others, I usually . . .
7. I feel most vulnerable during a conflict when . . .
8. On this team, we usually handle conflict by . . .
9. I usually hide or camouflage my feelings when . . .
10. When I get angry, I . . .
11. When someone avoids conflict with me, I . . .
12. I am most likely to assert myself in situations that . . .
13. My greatest strength in handling conflict is . . .
14. In this team, I would have the most difficulty with . . .
15. The most important outcome of conflict is . . .

Lecture Notes: **STYLES OF CONFLICT RESOLUTION**

1. **Denial.** "Conflict? What conflict? There is no conflict."

   Advantages: _____

   _____

   Disadvantages: _____

   _____

2. **Smoothing Over.** "Sure, we have some conflict, but it's no big deal. Everything is fine."

   Advantages: _____

   _____

   Disadvantages: _____

   _____

3. **Power.** "Since I have the authority, I'll decide."

   Advantages: _____

   _____

Disadvantages: _____

_____

4. **Compromise.** "Let's split the difference. You do this . . . and I'll do this."

    Advantages: _____

    _____

    Disadvantages: _____

    _____

5. **Collaboration.** "Let's you and I together figure out the problem and come up with the best solution for all concerned."

    Advantages: _____

    _____

    Disadvantages: _____

    _____

Activity 6

Creating a Team Logo

Purpose

1. To initiate or conclude a discussion of team values and purpose
2. To open or close a team-building or training workshop with an energizing activity

Group Size

Works best with an intact team of four to twelve people. The activity can be used in a team workshop when the group has been divided into teams.

Time

45 minutes to 1 hour

Physical Setting

For a team-building session, chairs are arranged in a circle or around a conference table. In a team-training workshop, use chairs and round or rectangular tables, spread out around the room.

Materials

Easel, flipchart, markers, and masking tape or push pins

Process

1. Explain that the purpose of the activity is to create a logo for the team. The logo is to represent the team's values and purpose as well as anything else that distinguishes the team. Suggest that participants begin the activity with a discussion of their values and purpose. The finished product is to be presented on a sheet of flipchart paper.
2. The team presents the logo, along with its rationale. In a team-training workshop, other teams can ask questions for clarification. The facilitator should ask the team to share their learnings from the experience, using the debriefing questions.
3. The team may elect to take the logo back to the workplace and use it in some fashion.

Debriefing

- How do you feel about the process used to develop the logo?
- To what extent were all team members involved?
- What did you learn about your teammates?
- Do you think the logo will reflect the team's goals and values one year from today? Three years? Five years?
- Does this exercise suggest some ways the team might need to change, grow, or develop?

Variations

1. Create a team slogan, song, or name.
2. Select a well-known song, movie, television show, or book title that reflects the team's purpose or values.

Activity 7

Creating a Team Mission

A Team-Development Activity

Purpose

1. To develop a shared view of a team's products or services
2. To develop a shared view of a team's customers
3. To create a team mission statement
4. To train participants in preparing a mission statement

Group Size

Works best with an intact team of four to eight people. In a team training workshop, the exercise can be done with up to fifteen people.

Time

1 hour

Physical Setting

Table and chairs arranged in U-shape

Materials

1. Easel, flipchart, markers, and masking tape or push pins
2. A copy of *Creating a Team Mission* for each person
3. A copy of *Evaluating a Team Mission* for each person

Process

1. Explain the purpose of the activity.
2. Lecture on the content of a mission statement. A mission statement describes a team's products or services and its customers. It answers the questions:

   • What do you do?
   • For whom do you do it?

   A mission statement can also reveal something about a team's values and its unique talents, or type of technology.
3. Write the name of the team on a flipchart. Ask the group to brainstorm words and phrases that describe the team.
4. Record the responses in an unorganized fashion on the flipchart. (Do not simply create a vertical list.)
5. Ask participants to use the handout *Creating a Team Mission* and write one or two sentences that describe the team's products or services and its customers. They should use the "brainstormed" list for ideas, but they should not be restricted to those particular words or phrases.
6. Ask one person to present his mission statement. Write the statement on the flipchart.
7. Ask the team to clarify, discuss, and edit the statement until it gets close to a consensus on the words. Do not try to produce a final product.
8. Using the handout *Evaluating a Team Mission*, ask the team to assess its statement against the criteria.
9. Conclude the session by telling participants that the draft statement will be typed and distributed to the team after the session.
10. At the next meeting, discuss the mission statement again and reach a consensus for the final version.

Debriefing

• How do you feel about the process used to come up with this mission?
• How satisfied are you with the team's mission statement?

- In what ways will the mission statement be useful to the team?
- How can we keep the mission a "living document" for our team?

Variations

1. Review the handout *Evaluating a Team Mission* prior to drafting the mission statement.
2. Ask a subcommittee to edit the draft after the session and to bring it to the next team meeting.
3. Ask each person to prepare a draft mission statement as a prework assignment and then to bring it to the session.

Worksheet

Creating a Team Mission

The mission of the team is to:

_____

_____

_____

_____

_____

_____

_____

_____

_____

_____

_____

_____

Worksheet

Evaluating a Team Mission

1. **Consistency:**   Is it consistent with the corporate mission?

   _____

   _____

2. **Brevity:**   Is it brief and to the point?

   _____

   _____

3. **Clarity:**   Is it easy to understand?

   _____

   _____

4. **Specific:**   Does it reflect the unique character and flavor of your team?

   _____

   _____

5. **General:**   Is it broad enough to include some growth and expansion of your products or services and your customer base?

   _____

   _____

6. **Pride:**   Are you proud of it? Would you frame it and hang it in your work area? Would you show it to your boss? Would you show it to your customers?

   _____

   _____

Activity 8

Customer Delight

A Data-Collection Tool

Purpose

1. To collect information on customer perceptions of the team
2. To create a plan for improving customer satisfaction

Group Size

The data-collection tool is designed for use in individual interviews with customers. It can also be used by a facilitator of a focus group composed of customers. An effective focus group consists of six to eight members. It might be necessary to eliminate some of the questions when using the tool in a focus group.

Time

An individual interview using the tool will take 45 minutes to 1 hour. A focus group should be scheduled for 1 to 1¹/₂ hours.

Physical Setting

An individual interview should be conducted in a private setting, such as small conference room or private office. A focus group should be held in a small conference room, with chairs set around a small rectangular table.

Materials

1. A copy of the *Customer Delight* tool for the interviewer as well as the customer.
2. A focus group facilitator will need a copy of the tool to guide the discussion.

Process

1. Explain the purpose of the interview, the confidentiality guidelines, and how the results will be used. Make it clear what the customer will see. The general rule is that a summary of the data is prepared, with no names associated with any of the ideas, comments, or recommendations. Similar guidelines apply to focus groups.
2. Give a copy of the tool to the interviewee. Explain that the participant can follow along, but that you will take notes on your copy.
3. Follow up each question with probes such as:

    - Can you tell me more about that?
    - How would that work?
    - Do you have any examples of that?
    - Help me understand why that is an issue.

4. Use your active listening skills to bring out more information, using comments such as:

    - So, you're saying . . .
    - In other words, the real issue is . . .
    - If I can summarize what you just said, you seem to feel that . . .
    - Therefore, your recommendation is that the team should . . .

5. At the conclusion of the interview, go back and review your notes with the interviewee to determine whether your notes are accurate. Remind the person what will happen with the information.

Debriefing

While we do not usually debrief an interview, if time permits, consider some of the following:

- How did you feel about the interview process?
- Were the questions I asked what you expected?
- Were there any surprises?

- Are there any questions that you expected to be asked that I didn't ask?
- Did you learn anything from this process?

Variations

1. If you are unable to use the interview method, consider a survey instrument. One such instrument is the *Customer Focus Survey,* a team self-assessment that measures the extent to which the team is customer focused. Another is the *Customer Perceptions Survey,* which collects data on the customer's perceptions of the extent of teamwork demonstrated during interactions with the team.*

2. If your time with the customer is limited, you can reduce the number of questions. We recommend using 1, 2, 4, 8, 9 and 10 for shorter interviews.

---

*Both instruments are found in Glenn M. Parker's *25 Instruments for Team Building,* published by HRD Press, 1998.

Worksheet

Customer Delight

Purpose: These questions are designed to solicit feedback from customers about how well the team is meeting their needs. All responses will remain confidential.

1. What are some of the ways the team collects information about your needs?

_____

_____

_____

2. How satisfied are you with the way the team collects information about your needs? What else should be done?

_____

_____

_____

3. How often does the team talk with you about your needs? Is this too often? Not often enough? How often would you recommend?

_____

_____

_____

4. How would you describe the way the team responds to your questions, requests for information, and complaints?

_____

_____

_____

5. How would you characterize your relationship with the team? Collaborative? Adversarial? Friendly? Competitive? A partnership?

_____

_____

_____

6. Does it appear to you that all members of the team are operating from the same guidelines? With the same goals? With the same quality standards? With the same concern for customer satisfaction?

_____

_____

_____

7. How would you describe meetings with the team? Well planned? Too long or short? Productive? What can be done to improve these meetings?

_____

_____

_____

8. When the team makes a mistake, misses a deadline, or in some other way does not meet expectations, how it is handled? What, if anything, would you like to see done differently?

_____

_____

_____

9. Given complete freedom of choice, would you continue to do business with this team? Why?

_____

_____

_____

10. What are some of the things the team can do to improve its relationship with you?

_____

_____

_____

Activity 9

Drawings

Improving Collaboration among Teams

Purpose

1. To assess the current state of collaboration among teams in an organization
2. To improve collaboration among teams in an organization

Group Size

Five to forty people in a team-building session

Time

2 hours

Physical Setting

A large room, with a round or rectangular table and chairs for each team

Materials

A set of the following materials for each team:

1. Book of drawing paper
2. Colored pens

3. Transparent tape
4. Blank paper

Process

1. Explain that the purpose of the activity is to reflect the current state of collaboration among teams in the organization using only a book of drawings, no words. Teams may only use the materials provided. One book is to be prepared per team, which will represent the combined efforts of all teams. Each team may only send one person at any time to another team to communicate about the project. There is a time limit of one hour.
2. At the conclusion of the activity, the drawings should be shared and discussed as a basis for identifying cross-team collaboration problems. The discussion should also bring out what was learned from working together on this project.
3. The facilitator should help the group develop a list of action items to address the problems.
4. The session should conclude with a lecture on the obstacles and strategies for effective interteam collaboration, as well as a general debriefing. You may use the lecture notes from Activity 45: Tricky Tales.

Debriefing

- How did it feel to give up your normal language for communication in favor of a pictorial mode?
- How did you share your personal drawings in the subgroups?
- Discuss the interaction within the subgroups
- What do the drawings tell you?
- Were you surprised by any of the drawings?
- What actions will you take as a result of this activity?

Variations

1. After problems have been identified, ask each team to analyze one of the problems and devise an action plan for it.
2. For related activities, see Activity 5: Communicating about Conflict: Learning Ways to Resolve Conflict.

Activity 10

E-Handles

A Closing Activity for a Mature Team

Purpose

1. To bring closure to a team-building intervention with an intact team
2. To provide positive feedback to teammates
3. To close a session in a fun and upbeat way

Group Size

Works best with an intact team of less than ten people

Time

30 to 45 minutes, depending on the size of the team. See variations for a way of reducing the time required.

Physical Setting

Chairs arranged in a circle or around a circular or rectangular table

Materials

1. Sufficient number of 3 × 5 cards
2. Flipchart and markers

Process

1. Introduce the activity as an upbeat and fun way to close a team-building experience. Remind the team of the "old days" before e-mail and car phones, when people had CB radios in their cars and trucks. Each person created a "handle" or name that they used to identify themselves to other CBers. These handles were often a description of their personality or occupation, such as "Texas Trainer." Today, e-mail addresses are often cold, formal variations of the person's name. In this exercise, you will have a chance to create e-mail addresses or handles with some warmth and personality for your teammates.

2. Explain that you are asking participants to create e-mail handles for their teammates. These handles should reflect only the most positive aspects of the person's style, role, skills, or experience. This is not the time for negative feedback.

3. Post some examples on the flipchart, such as:

   - Funone@disney.com
   - qualityguy@ge.com
   - rockindoc@merck.com
   - carebear@fda.gov
   - turnedontechie@microsoft.com

4. If time permits, ask team members to create an e-mail "handle" for every teammate. Allow 10 to 15 minutes, depending on how many people are participating. Each handle should be written on a 3 × 5 card.

5. You can either (a) collect the cards for each person in a separate envelope and give it to the person who, in turn, reads the handles, or (b) simply go around the team, one person at a time, and have teammates present their handles for the person.

6. Debrief the exercise, using some or all of the questions provided.

Debriefing

- How did you feel about this activity?
- How do you feel about yourself as a result of getting this feedback?
- Which handle did you like best? Why?
- Assuming the organization will allow it, would you ever consider using one of the handles as your email address?
- How did this activity help us as a team?
- If you were going to do this exercise with another team, how would you change it?
- How does positive feedback help us?

Variations

1. If you have less time available to you, write the names of all the team members on individual 3 × 5 cards and put the cards in a envelope. Ask participants to select one card from the envelope (but not their own) and write a handle for that person on the opposite side of the card. Then go around the team and have participants identify the person and the handle they created for that person.
2. Make a game of Variation 1 by asking the person to first read the handle and then ask the other people to guess for whom the handle was created.
3. Similarly, in Process Step 5 (a), after the person reads the handle on the card, ask him to guess who created the handle. Other team members can also guess.

Activity 11

Forming New Teams

A Get-Acquainted and Introductory Activity

Purpose

1. To quickly form new teams with strangers or people who do not usually work together
2. To learn factors that help and hinder team problem-solving and decision-making
3. To get acquainted with other participants at a conference or company meeting

---

Group Size

Any size group

Time

45 minutes to 1 hour

Physical Setting

Large room with movable chairs

Materials

1. Copies of the following for each person:

    - *Getting to Know You*
    - *The Things You Know You Know*
    - *Team Process Review*

2. Flipchart and markers or overhead projector, blank transparencies, and acetate marking pens

Process

1. Give each person a card with a name on it that is part of a pair of names. See *Ideas for Pairs* handout. Make sure that people who know each other are not paired.
2. Explain the purpose of the activity. Ask participants to take out their cards and find their partners.
3. Round 1: Once they find their partners, they are to use the *Getting to Know You* handout to facilitate their discussion. Allow 15 minutes.
4. Round 2: Ask the pairs to find another pair and then introduce their partners to each other, using the information from the handout. Allow 15 minutes.
5. Round 3: Distribute *The Things You Know You Know* handout. Explain that the task is to use their team resources to answer the questions. Allow 15 minutes.
6. When they have answered the questions, give participants copies of the *Team Process Review* and ask them to complete it.
7. The teams should use the form as a basis for discussion of factors that help and hinder team effectiveness.
8. Summarize the learnings from the team experience by first asking the group to share its answers to question 4 on the process review. The facilitator should add any points not sufficiently covered.
9. Distribute the answers to *The Things You Know You Know* questions.
10. Debrief the session, using some of the questions provided.

Debriefing

- How do you feel about this activity?
- What value did it add to you? To your team? To your understanding of teamwork?

- What would you have changed to make it a more useful experience for you?
- What did you learn?
- What surprised you?
- How will this help you?
- What will you do differently as a result of this experience?

Variations

1. Change *The Things You Know You Know* to questions about the company or industry, or a related topic.
2. Change the pairs to States and their Capitals.
3. In Step 4, ask the pairs to join with two other pairs to form a team of six people.
4. Make it a competitive exercise, with the first team to get all the correct answers declared the winner. Give the winning team a prize.
5. Change it to a get-acquainted activity by stopping at Step 3.
6. Eliminate the *Team Process Review.*
7. Other get-acquainted activities are Activity 50: Yea, Team! A Large-Group Icebreaker and Activity 21: Personal Ads: A Large-Group Icebreaker.

Worksheet

Ideas for Pairs

1. Romeo and Juliet
2. Abbott and Costello
3. Starsky and Hutch
4. Butch Cassidy and the Sundance Kid
5. Peanut Butter and Jelly
6. Joanne Woodward and Paul Newman
7. Cagney and Lacy
8. Bacon and Eggs
9. Dun and Bradstreet
10. Bricks and Mortar
11. King and Queen
12. Michael Jordan and Scottie Pippin
13. Laurel and Hardy
14. Rosencranz and Guildenstern
15. Minneapolis and St. Paul
16. Elizabeth Barrett and Robert Browning
17. Wile E.Coyote and Roadrunner
18. Mickey Mouse and Donald Duck
19. Will and Grace
20. Rogers and Hart
21. Sonny and Cher
22. Laverne and Shirley
23. Bonnie and Clyde
24. Ronald Reagan and George Bush
25. Simon and Garfunkel
26. Mork and Mindy
27. Anthony and Cleopatra
28. Tom Sawyer and Huckleberry Finn
29. Thelma and Louise
30. Felix Unger and Oscar Madison

Worksheet

Getting to Know You

The purpose of this meeting is to get to know the other person. Use these questions as a guide only. Feel free to ask and answer other questions that interest you. Take notes. In Round 2 you will be asked to introduce your partner to other people.

1. Where were you born? Where were you brought up?

   _____

   _____

   _____

2. What is your job? What do you like best about it? What would you change about it?

   _____

   _____

   _____

3. Tell me about your family.

   _____

   _____

   _____

4. What are your hobbies and outside interests?

   _____

   _____

   _____

5. Where did you go on your last vacation? Where are you going this year?

_____

_____

_____

6. If you could change occupations, what would you do?

_____

_____

_____

7. Other questions (How do you feel about this meeting? How do you feel about this exercise? What did you get out of this session? etc.).

_____

_____

The Things You Know You Know

1. What are the names of the thirteen original colonies?

_____

_____

_____

2. Who was Richard Nixon's running mate in 1960?

_____

_____

_____

3. Name the seven deadly sins.

_____

_____

_____

4. What are the names of the planets, beginning with the one closest to the sun?

_____

_____

_____

5. What is the longest river in the world, and what continent is it on?

_____

_____

_____

The Things You Know You Know Answer Sheet

1. The thirteen original colonies were:

Virginia	New Jersey
Maryland	Delaware
Massachusetts	Pennsylvania
Connecticut	North Carolina
New Hampshire	South Carolina
Rhode Island	Georgia
New York	

2. Richard Nixon's running mate in 1960 was Henry Cabot Lodge.

3. The seven deadly sins are:

Pride	Gluttony
Covetousness	Envy
Lust	Sloth
Anger	

4. The names of the planets are:

   Mercury
   Venus
   Earth
   Mars
   Jupiter
   Saturn
   Uranus
   Neptune
   Pluto

5. The longest river is the Nile, in Africa.

Worksheet

Team Process Review

1. What did your team do that helped complete the task?

   _____

   _____

   _____

   _____

2. What things hindered the completion of the task?

   _____

   _____

   _____

   _____

3. What would you do differently next time?

   _____

   _____

   _____

   _____

4. What did you learn about team effectiveness?

   _____

   _____

   _____

   _____

Activity 12

Freeze Frame

Dealing with Problem Behaviors in Teams

Purpose

1. To identify and describe behaviors that interfere with team effectiveness
2. To develop a set of interventions that minimize or eliminate the behaviors

Group Size

Fifteen to forty people in a team-training workshop

Time

1½ to 2 hours

Physical Setting

A room large enough for groups of five to eight people to work without overhearing each other; movable chairs and no tables

Materials

Easel, flipchart, markers, and masking tape or push pins

Process

1. Facilitator outlines the goals of the session and explains that the participants' actual experiences with problem behaviors will be used as data for learning, rather than hypothetical cases.
2. The facilitator asks participants to briefly describe behaviors they have observed that were counterproductive or difficult to handle (e.g., monopolizing,

wisecracking, attacking leader or agenda). One-line summaries of these behaviors are posted on the flipchart. Keep the list to eight or ten behaviors.

3. Using the consensus method, reduce the list to no less than three and no more than six behaviors, depending upon the size of the group. The two main criteria for reducing the list are: (1) behaviors that produce the most difficulty and (2) behaviors that occur most frequently.

4. The facilitator writes a short version of each behavior on a sheet of flipchart paper, one per sheet, and posts them in different sections of the room.

5. The facilitator explains that each person should select one behavior to work on, and move to the section of the room where the flipchart paper describing the behavior is posted. The groups that have now been formed complete the following task:

   - Discuss their experiences with and handling of the behavior.
   - Prepare a 2-minute vignette that depicts the behavior, with members of the group acting as:
     —Narrator (sets the stage by explaining who, when, where, etc.)
     —Facilitator (leads the vignette, and then pulls and processes the learning)
     —Group members (problem-behavior participants and others as required to simulate the event)
   - Present the vignette up to the point where the behavior occurs but before the facilitator intervenes. The frame freezes at this point.

6. Each group presents its vignette and stops when the behavior has been depicted. The facilitator in the group then asks participants from other groups to indicate how they would intervene at this point.

7. The facilitator leads the group in acting out some proposed interventions and posts ideas on the flipchart. The group also presents one or more of its own.

8. This format continues until all groups have presented their vignettes.

9. Debrief the session using some or all of the questions provided.

10. The facilitator concludes the session by identifying the interventions that are generally applicable to all situations, and then presenting ideas for handling problems. Use the handout from Activity 19: Meeting Monsters.

Debriefing

- How did you feel about the scenarios? Were they realistic?
- What did you learn from this experience?
- What things will you do differently in the future?
- What are the "universal truths" for handling problem team members?

Variation

For a less complex activity, see Activity 19: Meeting Monsters: Dealing with Problem People on Teams.

Activity 13

Got Culture?

A Team-Assessment Tool

Purpose

1. The purpose of this activity is to assess the culture of an intact team in order to determine how it can become more effective in general, and specifically in four areas:

   A. Role Clarity
   B. Respect
   C. Communication
   D. Reward System

2. The information can be used by the team to plan its future structure, problem-solve, or take advantage of opportunities.

Group Size

Works best with an intact team of any size

Time

Depending on the size of the group, this activity can take up to 4 hours. The survey takes approximately 30 minutes to complete.

Physical Setting

A space large enough for participants to complete the survey and then work in small groups to problem-solve and create action plans.

Materials

1. A copy of *The Team Culture Survey* for each participant
2. A copy of *The Team Culture Survey Scoring and Interpretation Guide* for each participant

3. Easel, flipchart, markers, and masking tape or push pins
4. A copy of the *Multivoting Guidelines* for each participant

Process

1. The facilitator explains the purpose of the activity as an opportunity to take stock of the team's "culture," and to create plans to change it if necessary.
2. The facilitator distributes copies of the survey and directs participants to complete it (including scoring their instrument). Allow 30 minutes for this task.
3. Once everyone has completed and scored the instruments, the facilitator hands out the *Team Culture Scoring and Interpretation Guide.*
4. All members should review their scores and then form subgroups (or form one large group if the total size is less than eight). The facilitator asks them to share their scores and create a group score for each item and one for each category. Space is provided on the scoring sheet for this task.
5. Once the scores are determined, the group should engage in an analysis of the results to find common areas of concern and opportunity. Allow 45 minutes for this task.
6. Ask each group to present its findings. Bring the whole team back together and start the presentations. Allow 15 minutes for this task.
7. The facilitator should post the common issues, concerns, and opportunities and seek agreement about their priority by using multivoting. After the top three or four have been identified, each subgroup is assigned a concern or issue to analyze. Allow 45 minutes for this task.
8. Once the analysis phase is complete, have each team present its analysis. Conduct a general discussion on each issue. Allow 45 minutes for this task.
9. Bring the groups back together and ask participants to prepare action plans to deal with their concern. Allow 15 minutes.
10. Debrief, using the questions below.

Debriefing

- What was the value of this activity?
- How will this new data help us become a high performing team?
- What insights do these questions and responses provide?

Variation

The facilitator can score the survey and prepare a written report prior to the working session.

Worksheet

The Team Culture Survey

Instructions: Read each item carefully. Then rate how much you *agree* with each item, using the five-point scale below. Record your rating in the space provided to the left of the item.

> 5. Strongly agree
> 4. Agree
> 3. Neither agree nor disagree
> 2. Disagree
> 1. Strongly disagree

After you have rated your agreement with each of the items, then rate each item on how important you think it is to your organization's success, using the five-point scale below. Record your rating in the space provided to the right of each item.

> 5. Critically Important
> 4. Very Important
> 3. Important
> 2. Somewhat Unimportant
> 1. Unimportant

	Agreement Rating	Importance Rating

A. Role Clarity

	Agreement Rating	Importance Rating
1. Our team has clear goals and objectives.	_____	_____
2. Our team is clear about priorities.	_____	_____
3. We know what our responsibilities are.	_____	_____
4. We know exactly what is expected of us.	_____	_____
5. I know what most people in the company do.	_____	_____
6. Work on this team makes the best use of people's experience.	_____	_____
7. I know what most people around me do.	_____	_____

     8. I know what most other departments do.   ————————   ————————

     9. The company has good, quality workers.   ————————   ————————

B. Respect

   10. I feel valued by my colleagues on the team.   ————————   ————————

   11. I value my colleagues on the team.   ————————   ————————

   12. I feel valued by my colleagues in the   ————————   ————————
       company as a whole.

   13. I value my colleagues in the company as a   ————————   ————————
       whole.

   14. My team respects other departments.   ————————   ————————

   15. My team is respected by other   ————————   ————————
       departments.

C. Communication

   16. We receive all the information we need to   ————————   ————————
       carry out our work.

   17. People on this team do not spend too   ————————   ————————
       much time on the unessential.

   18. I am kept adequately informed about   ————————   ————————
       significant issues in the company as a
       whole.

   19. I am kept appropriately informed through   ————————   ————————
       the "grapevine" and other informal
       means.

   20. My team works well with other teams or   ————————   ————————
       departments.

   21. My team receives all the information it   ————————   ————————
       needs to carry out its function well.

   22. My team is kept adequately informed   ————————   ————————
       about significant issues in the company as
       a whole.

   23. I understand clearly how I can contribute   ————————   ————————
       to the general goals of the company.

   24. I have adequate opportunities to express   ————————   ————————
       my views in my team.

   25. My colleagues are generally eager to   ————————   ————————
       discuss work matters with me.

   26. In general, communication is effective in   ————————   ————————
       this team.

   27. I work effectively because other team   ————————   ————————
       members communicate regularly with me.

D. Reward System

28. Good work is recognized appropriately.   _____ _____

29. I think my team leader is too tolerant of   _____ _____
poor performers.

30. Work that is not of the highest importance   _____ _____
is dealt with appropriately on my team.

31. In general, people are adequately rewarded   _____ _____
on this team.

32. In my opinion, the team's pay scale is   _____ _____
competitive with similar companies.

33. I receive an appropriate salary.   _____ _____

34. I receive appropriate benefits.   _____ _____

35. There is an appropriate difference between   _____ _____
the pay awarded to good team performers
and that awarded to bad performers.

36. I feel a strong sense of job satisfaction.   _____ _____

Worksheet

The Team Culture Survey Scoring and Interpretation Guide

Instructions: Collect all of the team members' scores and create a mean (average) for both the *Agreement* rating and the *Importance* rating for all survey items. You can also create a mean for the four categories: role clarity, respect, communication, and reward system. Use a blank copy of the survey to create your team means.

Interpretation

1. A High score is a mean of 3.5 or higher. A Low score is a mean of 3.4 or lower.
2. A High score in both Agreement and Importance signals *strength*. In other words, you believe the item is important for your success, and you do it well.
3. A High score in Importance and a Low score in Agreement indicate a *weakness* or an *area for improvement*. In other words, you see the item as important for your success but you do not do it well.
4. As a team, first look at your strengths and decide what you do now that is positive and should be continued.
5. Then, look at your areas for improvement and decide what you need to do to improve the situation.
6. Develop an action plan to increase your team's effectiveness, based on the survey results.

Worksheet — *Multivoting Guidelines*

Purpose: This tool helps a group quickly prioritize a list of items. It identifies which items are considered most urgent or promising by the group, using multiple votes.

Procedure

1. Count the items on the list (e.g., 36 items).
2. Divide the total by three (e.g., 36/3 = 12).
3. Team members individually select the [12] items they like best (only one vote per item).
4. By a show of hands, tally the number of votes per item. Write the number next to the item on the flipchart.
5. Circle the top priorities, or write them on a separate sheet of flipchart paper.

Variation

Alternatively, you can use stick-on red dots. Give each person as many dots as the number identified in Step 2.

Each person votes by placing a dot next to a concern on the flipchart. Tally the dots to rank the list.

Activity 14

Get SMART

Goal-Setting Skill Development

Purpose

1. To learn the SMART protocol for preparing team goals
2. To write team goals that follow the SMART protocol

Group Size

This activity works best with a group of six to eight people. If the class is larger, additional subgroups can be created.

Time

30 minutes

Physical Setting

Circles set around a round or rectangular table

Materials

1. A copy of *Team Goals Are SMART* for each participant
2. A copy of the *Team Goals Task* for each person
3. An overhead transparency of *SMART Goals*
4. A copy of *SMART Goal Examples* for each participant
5. An overhead projector and screen

Process

1. Open the session by pointing out the importance of effective team goals. Note that in a study of fifty teams in thirty different companies reported in *The Wisdom of Teams* by Jon Katzenbach and Douglas Smith, it was found that having clear performance objectives was the single most important factor distinguishing high-performing teams from all other teams.*

2. Distribute the handout *Team Goals Are SMART* to everyone. Also display it as a transparency on the overhead. Review the five components of the protocol, providing or asking the group for examples of each.

3. Distribute the *Team Goals Task* handout to everyone. Ask each person to complete the task. Allow 3 minutes. Then ask the group to review each person's contribution and arrive at a consensus on a goal that meets the SMART guidelines. Allow 7 minutes.

4. Ask each group to write their consensus goal on a flipchart sheet and post it on the wall. Ask everyone to walk around and view the SMART "exhibit."

5. Distribute the *SMART Goal Examples* and discuss.

6. Debrief the session.

Debriefing

- Not looking at the handout, name the SMART protocol components.
- Why is it important for a goal to be specific? Measurable? Attainable? Relevant? Time-bound?
- What is the most difficult component to implement?
- Is everything a team does "measurable"?
- How do SMART goals help a team be successful?
- What is the most important thing to remember about goal-setting?
- How or when will you apply the learnings from this activity?
- What payoff do you expect from the SMART protocol?

Variations

1. Ask team members to write their goal on 3 × 5 cards. Collect the cards, shuffle them, and place them face down on the table. Then ask participants to select a card. If they select their own card, place it on the bottom of the deck and select again. They should review the goal for its alignment with the SMART guidelines and provide feedback on the card on how to improve the goal. All cards are returned to the deck. The cards are then returned to the original author, who revises the goal based on the feedback.

2. Use a sample goal that is relevant to your business.

*Jon Katzenbach and Douglas Smith, *The Wisdom of Teams,* Harvard Business School Press, Boston, 1993.

Worksheet

Team Goals are SMART

Specific . . .   The outcome or end result is very clear to everyone.

Measurable . . .   You can tell if you have achieved your goal because you can count it or see it.

Attainable . . .   While achieving the outcome might be a challenge, it is possible with the current team and resources.

Relevant . . .   The goal is in line with the direction provided by senior management, and it supports the strategy of the business.

Time-Bound . . .   All objectives must be achieved within a particular time period, such as "by the end of the third quarter" or by a specific date, such as June 30.

Worksheet

Team Goals Task

Task

Here is an ineffective goal. Your task is to rewrite it to conform to the SMART Goals protocol. First, complete the task individually. Then share the results with your teammates and develop a consensus on a team goal that meets the SMART guidelines.

Sample Goal

Improve the operations of the Customer Service Center.

_____

_____

_____

_____

_____

_____

_____

_____

_____

_____

_____

_____

_____

_____

SMART Goal Examples

1. By June 30, all calls to the Northeast Customer Service Team will be answered on the first ring.

2. By the end of the third quarter, 90 percent of all requests from customers will be handled within 48 hours.

Activity 15

How Do You Like to Receive Recognition?*

A Self-Assessment

Purpose

1. To give team members an opportunity to understand what types of recognition they value
2. To give team members an opportunity to learn what motivates their teammates
3. To help team members and others tailor their recognition more specifically to the needs of their teammates

Group Size

Most useful as an exercise for an intact team of ten or less. However, it can be used in a team-training class of twenty to thirty people. It can even be adapted for use with larger groups that are divided into small subgroups.

Time

1 hour

Physical Setting

Chairs around a round or rectangular table for an intact team. For a large group, clusters of chairs and tables set around the room.

*Reprinted from S. Thiagarajan and G. Parker, *Teamwork and Teamplay: Games and Activities for Building and Training Teams*. Copyright © 1999 by Jossey-Bass/Pfeiffer. Reprinted by permission of Jossey-Bass, Inc., *a subsidiary of John Wiley & Sons, Inc.*

Materials

1. One copy of *How Do You Like to Receive Recognition?* for each person
2. One copy of *How Do You Like to Receive Recognition? Score Sheet* for each participant

Process

1. Explain the purpose of the activity.
2. Distribute *How Do You Like to Receive Recognition?* to each person. Ask participants to complete the survey individually.
3. Distribute the *How Do You Like to Receive Recognition? Score Sheet* and ask each person to complete the form.
4. Present a lecture on the difference between intrinsic and extrinsic motivation. Explain that extrinsic factors are forms of recognition that come from outside the person and appeal to their outer-directed self. Intrinsic motivators appeal to the inner self, as they focus on things that might only be important to that particular person. They both have their place, and one is not better than the other. You might want to refer to a basic psychology text for more background on motivation prior to conducting this session.
5. With an intact team, ask participants to share their results and talk more specifically about what motivates and what demotivates them and why certain things would be especially appealing while others would be a real turn-off. If possible, ask people to share some examples of recognition they have received in the past and how they reacted to it.
6. Debrief the activity by asking what people learned and how they can put this learning to use.

Debriefing

- What did you learn about yourself as a result of this activity?
- What did you learn about your teammates?
- What did you learn about recognition? About motivation?
- How will this change the way you interact with your teammates?
- In what ways should the team change the ways it recognizes outstanding performance?
- What norms should we add to our list as a result of this activity?
- What implications does this activity have for our organization's reward and recognition program?
- What information should we give to our manager or sponsor about recognition?

Variations

1. It might be fun and useful to obtain a team score for extrinsic and intrinsic rewards. Add all the individual scores, and divide this number by the number of participants to get a team average for intrinsic and extrinsic forms of recognition. Use these results as the basis for a discussion on forms of recognition for the team as a whole.

2. If time is short, ask people to fill out the survey as prework for the session.

How Do You Like to Receive Recognition?

Instructions: Please review the following list of forms of recognition. Check the forms that you value and would like to receive. You may check as many as you like, but only check the ones that appeal to you.

_____ 1. To receive positive verbal feedback at a staff meeting

_____ 2. To be asked to take on a tough problem or a new challenge

_____ 3. To be asked to give a presentation on your work at a staff meeting or a company conference

_____ 4. To receive positive, handwritten comments in the margin of a document you prepared

_____ 5. To be invited to a barbecue or dinner party at the home of your boss

_____ 6. To be given the opportunity to work flexible hours or work at home

_____ 7. To attend a golf or tennis weekend at a beautiful resort with other award winners from the organization

_____ 8. To be given the opportunity to purchase new tools and equipment to enhance your work

_____ 9. To have your picture and a story about your work appear in the company or community newspaper

_____ 10. To be asked for your opinion on a difficult organizational problem or a new business opportunity

_____ 11. To be given the opportunity to speak about your work at an important professional conference

_____ 12. To be offered the opportunity to learn a new system or operate some new equipment, or in other ways increase your skills and knowledge

_____ 13. To have your picture displayed in a prominent location along with either letters of commendation

_____ 14. To be asked to help a colleague get started with a project or solve a particularly difficult problem

_____ 15. To receive verbal recognition for your work from a senior-level executive at a company forum attended by you and your colleagues

_____ 16. A solution that you recommended is implemented throughout the organization

_____ 17. A customer or other stakeholder sends a letter to your boss, praising your work

_____ 18. When you ask for help, your boss offers to pick up some of the load directly, share expertise, or obtain outside assistance

_____ 19. To be presented with a T-shirt, hat, or mug with your name or other indication on it that makes it clear that it is recognition for your work

_____ 20. To be empowered to make decisions, or to be able to act in other ways that increase control over your work

How Do You Like To Receive Recognition? Score Sheet

Instructions: Please transfer your responses to the columns below by placing a check beside the same numbers you checked on the survey, and then tally the columns.

Extrinsic rewards or recognition	Intrinsic rewards or recognition
1. _____	2. _____
3. _____	4. _____
5. _____	6. _____
7. _____	8. _____
9. _____	10. _____
11. _____	12. _____
13. _____	14. _____
15. _____	16. _____
17. _____	18. _____
19. _____	20. _____
Total = _____	Total = _____

Activity 16

How's Your Team's Vision?

A Team-Development Activity

Purpose

1. To assess the focus of the team
2. To develop the first two stages of a strategic planning process

Group Size

Works best with intact teams of fewer than ten, but can be used for larger groups by creating subgroups focused on specific elements of the plan

Time

4 hours

Physical Setting

Space large enough for the group to post flipcharts for reports and other information

Materials

1. Easel, flipchart, markers, and masking tape or push pins
2. A copy of the *Strategic Planning Process* handout for each participant
3. A copy of the *Tactical Action Planner* for each person

Process

1. The facilitator begins by explaining the purpose of the activity and presenting a brief overview of the strategic planning process.
2. The facilitator provides a copy of the *Strategic Planning Process* to each participant
3. The facilitator explains to the team that the first phase of the strategic planning process is to create a compelling vision of the future: What is it that you hope you will become?
4. The facilitator then asks each member to write one sentence that captures the vision of the team as they see it. These sentences should be written on flipchart paper and posted on the walls. Allow 15 to 20 minutes for this phase.
5. Once the statements have been posted, the group is directed to move around the room and read each statement. Allow 5 minutes for this activity.
6. Once the review process has been completed, the group reconvenes and the facilitator leads a discussion about the statements. The following process questions can be used to guide the discussion:

    *   How do you react to the statements?
    *   How close to your vision were the other statements?
    *   How close is this team to realizing the vision statements?

7. Using information from the discussion, the facilitator leads the group in the process of synthesizing the various statements into a single usable one. If there are subgroups working, the facilitator asks each group to synthesize its work and the process is repeated until all subgroups have integrated their statements into one statement.
8. Having achieved consensus on the statement (which should be posted), the facilitator asks the group to evaluate—on a scale of 0 to 10—how close they are to realizing their vision. This should be accomplished by having each member go to the flipchart and mark their rank on a scale of 0 to 10.

    Post the following scale on the flipchart:

    How close are we to achieving our vision?
    1. We are nowhere.
    2.
    3. We are making progress.
    4.
    5. We are halfway there.
    6.

       7. We are getting close.

       8.

       9.

    10. We are there.

9. The facilitator then gives the overall rank by taking an average of the individual scores and then conducts a planning session intended to develop tactics to move the overall score closer to 10.

10. Using the *Tactical Action Planner,* the team develops an action plan and sets a time and date to follow-up.

11. Debrief the activity, using the questions provided.

Debriefing

- What did you learn from this activity? Did you learn anything about yourself? Your teammates? The overall team?
- How do you feel about the product of the activity? Are you proud of it? Would you be willing to share it with senior management? Customers? Other stakeholders?
- How useful is this activity in helping the team evaluate its current position?
- How will this activity help the team move to the next steps in the strategic planning model?
- Conclude by reviewing the group's commitment and reinforcing the next meeting time and date.

Variations

1. Have the team members evaluate their effectiveness in advance.
2. Have the team members prepare vision statements prior to the session's start.
3. A companion exercise is Activity 7: Creating a Team Mission: A Team-Development Activity.

Strategic Planning Process

The strategic planning process is a process by which you formulate a connection among strategic, organizational, and tactical objectives.

1. **Visioning** involves a belief that aspects of the future can be influenced and changed by what we do now.
2. **Culture and applied strategic planning** creates an alignment between culture and vision that is required to facilitate focused growth.
3. **Planning to plan** sets the stage within the organization to support a planning process.
4. **Environmental monitoring** focuses on macro, industry, competitive, and internal factors that affect your organization.
5. **Values** involves stakeholder beliefs and alignment.
6. **Formulating a mission statement** maintains focus on the strategic direction of the organization.
7. **Business modeling** defines the performance targets, lines of business, and the critical success indicators relative to the organizational thrust.
8. **Performance audits** assess the organization's strengths, weaknesses, opportunities, and threats relative to existing business strategies.
9. **Gap analysis** identifies current gaps within the performance of existing lines of business and their strategic objectives.
10. **Integrating action plans** helps to develop the grand strategies needed to position your organization.
11. **Contingency planning** manages the risk associated with your plan, and prepares corrective actions.
12. **Implementation** moves the plan from purpose and vision to action.

Worksheet

Tactical Action Planner

What do we *need* to do in order to move closer to our vision? Identify tactics in each of the following areas:

1. Human Resources

   _____

   _____

   _____

2. Leadership and Management

   _____

   _____

   _____

3. Quality

   _____

   _____

   _____

4. Customer Service

   _____

   _____

   _____

5. Technology

   _____

   _____

   _____

Activity 17

Improving Team Meetings

Purpose

1. To learn the factors involved in a successful team meeting
2. To assess the current strengths of your team meetings
3. To develop a plan for improving your team meetings

Group Size

Works best with an intact team of four to twelve people. The activity can be adapted to a team-training workshop for a larger group.

Time

2 hours

Physical Setting

Conference table with chairs for a session with an intact team. The room arrangement for a training workshop will depend on the size of the group.

Materials

A copy of the *The Team Meeting Survey* for each participant

Process

1. Prior to the session, ask each team member to complete the *The Team Meeting Survey.*
2. Share and discuss the results.
3. Identify the key items that need to be improved. Develop a series of action plans to address the key items.
4. Summarize the meeting and identify next steps.

Variations

1. Revise the survey or use only a portion of it.
2. The facilitator can observe a team meeting and include observations on specific aspects of actions in the diagnosis.
3. Use the results as the basis for a team meeting.
4. For a more comprehensive team meeting survey tool, see "Team Meeting Assessment" in G. M. Parker, *25 Instruments for Team Building*, HRD Press, 1998.

The Team Meeting Survey

Please think about the way your team conducts meetings. Using the following scale, assess the extent to which these statements are true. Circle the number that best correponds with your thinking.

STATEMENTS	ALMOST NEVER	RARELY	SOMETIMES	OFTEN	ALMOST ALWAYS
1. Meetings are held only when necessary.	1	2	3	4	5
2. Effective use is made of nonmeeting methods (e.g.,conference calls).	1	2	3	4	5
3. There is an agenda for the meeting.	1	2	3	4	5
4. Participants receive the agenda prior to the meeting.	1	2	3	4	5
5. Agenda topics are sufficiently clear and specific.	1	2	3	4	5
6. Each agenda item specifies the time allocated to it.	1	2	3	4	5
7. Each agenda item specifies the person responsible for it.	1	2	3	4	5
8. The meeting notice includes the time the meeting will end.	1	2	3	4	5
9. The meeting notice specifies the prework required for the meeting.	1	2	3	4	5
10. The agenda specifies the action required on each item.	1	2	3	4	5
11. Only necessary and appropriate people attend the meeting.	1	2	3	4	5
12. Where possible, meetings are scheduled at the best possible time (i.e., time of day, day of week).	1	2	3	4	5

Activity 18

It's a Puzzlement

A Get-Acquainted Icebreaker

Purpose

1. To help participants in a team-training seminar get to know each other
2. To introduce some team concepts to participants in a team-training seminar
3. To form teams in a team-training seminar

Group Size

Designed for a team-training seminar group of up to twenty participants. If more participants are added to the group, additional puzzle parts will be needed.

Time

30 to 45 minutes

Physical Setting

Chairs around a table, with sufficient space around the room to allow for easy movement of the participants

Materials

1. Sufficient number of puzzle pieces so that each participant will have one part

2. Sufficient number of small envelopes (each puzzle part needs envelope)
3. A copy of the *"It's a Puzzlement" Discussion Guide* for each person
4. Flipchart and markers

Process

1. Prior to the session, prepare the puzzle parts. Be certain to only use matched sets of parts (e.g., the title or name and its description or definition). If there is an odd number of participants, you should participate in the activity to even it out. Place each puzzle piece in an envelope.
2. As participants enter the room (or at some other appropriate time), give each person an envelope containing one puzzle part.
3. Distribute the guidelines. Review Round 1 instructions. Ask people to find their partner and begin the discussion. Allow 7 minutes.
4. Stop the discussion and refer the participants to the instructions for Round 2. Ask people to form groups of four and begin the discussion. Allow 10 minutes.
5. Ask people to stay in their groups. You may wish to give them another set of questions to discuss that pertain to the subject matter of the seminar, or a brief team problem to solve.
6. Debrief the activity using some or all of the questions provided.

Debriefing

- How did you feel about meeting new people in this way?
- What did you learn that was useful about the other people? About yourself? About teams?
- In what ways can you apply what you learned?
- What more would you like to know about the other people? About teams?

Variations

1. Change the puzzle parts to topics in your course or about your company (especially useful in a new-employee orientation class).
2. Add new puzzle parts so that the participants can repeat Round 1 with another person. A similar variation involves giving each person two puzzle parts in the envelope.
3. After Round 2, give the groups one of the other activities in this book to complete as a team.

Worksheet

"It's a Puzzlement" Puzzle Pieces

Instructions: Type or write the following on puzzle-part shapes that connect to each other. Do not include the numbers.

1. Ad hoc team that comes together to achieve a goal and then disbands.

2. A famous television show about a blended family team.

3. Team that works together but rarely if ever meets face-to-face.

4. A television show about a team of high-tech specialists headed by a leader known only as Mr. Phelps.

5. A decision that all team members can "live with."

6. The behavioral expectations or rules that guide and shape team member participation.

7. Basketball team that won six world championships in the 1990s.

8. Liverpool musical group that took the world by storm in the 1960s.

9. A team of people who work in different departments or represent different disciplines.

10. A long-running television show about a lovable team of varied characters who spend most of their time hanging out in a neighborhood bar in Boston.

1. Project Team

2. The Brady Bunch

3. Virtual Team

4. Mission Impossible

5. Consensus

6. Norms

7. Chicago Bulls

8. The Beatles

9. Cross-Functional Team

10. Cheers

"It's a Puzzlement" Discussion Guide

Round 1

Instructions: When you find your puzzle-part partner, use some or all of the following questions to get to know each other better:

For entertainment and sports teams (e.g., Beatles)

- Would you describe the group as a "team"?
- What are the defining characteristics of this team?
- What do you personally like about this team?
- Anything you dislike?
- In what ways was this team successful (beyond the fact that it enjoyed popular success)?
- In what ways was the group unsuccessful?
- What did it do well?
- What can we learn from this team?

For team concepts (e.g., consensus)

- Have you ever been a member of this type of team (e.g., project team)?
- Have you ever used this tool (norms)?
- What was your experience like?
- How successful was it?
- What worked well?
- What didn't work out so well?
- What did you learn from the experience?
- How have you applied the learnings?

Round 2

Team up with a group of four people, and use some or all of the following questions to guide your discussion:

- What's been your best experience as a team member? What made it special? What did you learn?
- What's been your worst team experience? What did you learn from that experience?
- What do you hope to learn today?
- What do you hope to walk away with from today's experience?
- What concerns or questions do you have about today's experience?
- What do you feel good about in terms of today's experience?

Puzzle Parts

An ad hoc team of people that comes together to solve a problem or achieve some other goal and then disband.	Project Team
A famous television show about a blended family team.	The Brady Bunch
A team of people who work together but never or only rarely have a face-to-face meeting.	Virtual Team
A television show about a team of high-tech specialist headed by a leader known only as Mr. Phelps	Mission Impossible
A decision that all team members can "live with."	Consensus
The behavioral expectations or rules that guide and shape team member participation.	Norms
The basketball team that won six world championships in the 1990s.	Chicago Bulls
The musical group from Liverpool that took the world by storm during the 1960s.	The Beatles
A team of people who work in different departments or represent different disciplines.	Cross-Functional Team
A long-running television show about a lovable team of varied characters who spend most of their time hanging out in a neighborhood bar in Boston.	Cheers

Activity 19

Meeting Monsters

Dealing with Problem People on Teams

Purpose

1. To identify the types of behavior that prevent effective team meetings
2. To develop specific techniques for dealing with problem people on your team

---

Group Size

Since this activity is designed for a team-training workshop, the size of the group is limited only by the space available and the ability of the leader to handle large groups. It works best with a group of up to twenty participants.

Time

1 to 1½ hours

Physical Setting

Table and chairs arranged in seminar style or in a U-shape

Materials

1. A copy of *Handling Problem Behaviors in Team Meetings* for each person
2. A copy of *Dealing with Dysfunctional Behavior in Team Meetings* for each participant

Process

1. Explain the purpose of the activity and distribute *Handling Problem Behaviors in Team Meetings*. Ask each person to complete the exercise alone.
2. Ask for volunteers to indicate how they would handle each type of behavior. Probe for specific words or actions. Paraphrase their responses to let them hear how it sounds.
3. Debrief the activity using some of the questions provided.
4. Conclude the session by presenting a list of interventions for dealing with dysfunctional behavior in groups. Use the handout *Dealing with Dysfunctional Behavior in Team Meetings.*

Debriefing

- Which of these behaviors have you encountered on your team?
- What other problem behaviors have you encountered?
- Which of these behaviors do you find most difficult to deal with?
- To what extent do you feel comfortable using the interventions that have been suggested?
- What has been the most important thing you have learned from this exercise?

Variations

1. Form subteams and assign one or two behaviors to each team to discuss and develop interventions.
2. Simulate a team meeting and ask participants to role-play several of the behaviors. Other team members are asked to respond to the problem behavior during the role-play.
3. One related activity that might help is Activity 12: Freeze Frame: Dealing with Problem Behaviors in Teams.

Worksheet

Handling Problem Behaviors in Team Meetings

Problem behaviors	*What would you say or do?*
1. Silence—member does not participate	
2. Overly long comment	
3. Too much humor or wisecracking	
4. Consistently arrives late	
5. Consistently leaves before the meeting is over	
6. Sidetracking—comments are way off subject	
7. Rushes team to a quick decision or to end the meeting too fast	
8. Engages in side conversations	
9. Monopolizes the discussion	
10. Introduces a personal problem or concern	

Worksheet

Dealing with Dysfunctional Behavior in Team Meetings

The following suggestions should help you deal with behavior that prevents the team from being effective:

- **Listen.** Maybe, just maybe, the person has a point. What you think of as dysfunctional behavior might just be your inability to appreciate a person with a different style. Use your active listening skills such as paraphrasing, questioning, and summarizing to identify the real issue.

- **Meet privately.** Probe to uncover the real causes of the resistance or negative behavior. Perhaps the person engages in this behavior because of work overload or perhaps there is a mismatch between the person's skill set and the assignment.

- **Reestablish team norms.** This approach is recommended when there are several people who are exhibiting dysfunctional behavior. If your team does not have norms, developing a list often leads to a discussion of the extent to which the norms are being followed. If your team has existing norms, identify them and facilitate a discussion on their current relevance, as well as possible additions to the list, and the importance of adhering to the norms.

- **Negotiate.** Sometimes you can neutralize dysfunctional behavior by agreeing to a trade-off. For example, "If you agree to back off on the ethical issue until we complete work on our mission statement today, I will make sure we spend time on the ethical question at the beginning of our next meeting."

- **Positive reinforcement.** If the person does make a useful contribution, give positive feedback. For example, when "Silent Sam" spoke up and asked, "What's the point of this discussion?" the leader responded with "That's a good question, Sam, thanks . . ."

- **Confront the person.** Actually, the point is to confront the behavior, not the person. Although this is best done in private, sometimes direct feedback during a meeting is necessary. You must be specific and point to the person's behavior. For example, "Stan, your insistence that we collect more data is slowing us down, causing us to miss deadlines and renege on commitments to clients."

Activity 20

My Team and Me

Increasing Team Members' Identification with the Team

Purpose

To help a team identify those factors that affect the degree of positive identification with the team and its purpose

Group Size

Unlimited. This activity is designed for use with an intact work team.

Time

1 hour

Physical Setting

A space large enough for the team to work comfortably and to be able to post their work for each member to view

Materials

1. A copy of the *Team Identification Model (TIM)* for each participant
2. A copy of *The Team Identification Model Scoring Instructions* for each participant.
3. Easel, flipcharts, and masking tape or push pins

Process

1. The team leader hands out copies of the *Team Identification Model (TIM)*.
2. Team members are asked to read the instructions and complete the TIM.
3. The team leader hands out copies of *The Team Identification Model Scoring Instructions*. Team members score the TIM.
4. Once participants have completed the TIM, they post them on the wall and walk around to view the work of other members.
5. The team reassembles for a discussion that seeks to clarify and analyze the various responses.
6. With the leader, team members develop ways to help increase identification with the team.

Debriefing

- What can we do as a group to forge greater identification among team members?
- What can we do as individuals to forge greater identification with the team?
- How did this activity help you determine the effect of identification on your team's ability to be successful?

Team Identification Model (TIM)

Instructions: The *TIM Form* is composed of ten beliefs that reflect an individual team member's identification with the purpose and goals of the team. The level of strength of each belief can help enhance or detract from an individual team member's identification with the team's goals.

1. Review each of the ten beliefs below.
2. For each belief, assign a strength value. (One for a weak belief, and five for a strong belief.)

TIM Statements	**Belief Strength Scale**				
	Weak			*Strong*	
1. My belief in the team's overall purpose	1	2	3	4	5
2. My belief in the team's ability to achieve its purpose	1	2	3	4	5
3. My belief in the team's willingness to support fellow members	1	2	3	4	5
4. My belief that the team is able to be self-directed and self-renewing	1	2	3	4	5
5. My belief in the team-development process	1	2	3	4	5
6. My belief in the team's current working objectives	1	2	3	4	5
7. My belief that the rest of the organization perceives the team positively	1	2	3	4	5
8. My belief in the team's link to the wider organizational goals	1	2	3	4	5
9. My belief that there is a clear match between the team's goals and my personal goals	1	2	3	4	5
10. My belief in the leader's willingness to support team members	1	2	3	4	5

Total points for the ten questions _____

Worksheet

The Team Identification Model Scoring Instructions

The Team Identification Model is designed to help a team identify those factors that affect a team member's sense of identification with the team's purpose, goals, process, members, and so on—as well as that person's willingness to fully participate in the team's work.

The maximum possible score is fifty, which would indicate that the respondent believes very strongly in all ten beliefs. The minimum score is ten, which indicates that the respondent holds little or no identification with the team and its purpose.

The following scale will provide some focus for action and reflection:

1. Little or no identification ....10 points to 15 points
2. Some identification ....16 points to 25 points
3. Moderate identification ....26 points to 35 points
4. Strong identification ....36 points to 45 points
5. Complete identification ....46 points to 50 points

Members who score either little or some identification need to reflect on their membership and reevaluate it. People with scores in the moderate range need to evaluate what must be done to move to the ideal range of strong and complete identification. Scores in the strong and complete range should reflect on what must be done to maintain these levels.

Activity 21

Personal Ads

A Large-Group Icebreaker

Purpose

1. To facilitate interaction in a group of strangers
2. To help people get to know each other better
3. To form teams in an open enrollment team-training workshop
4. To help people understand the value of similarity and diversity in teams

Group Size

Works best with a group of at least eighteen people, although it can be used with a smaller group. It is also an effective kick-off exercise at a large conference.

Time

1 hour

Physical Setting

Large open space where a group can easily mingle, away from tables and chairs

Materials

1. Poster boards, markers, string, tape, scissors, pins, and other materials to prepare a poster of each person's personal ad

2. Flipchart and markers
3. One copy of *Personal Ad Descriptors* for each person
4. One copy of the *Sample Personal Ad* for each person
5. One copy of the *Personal Ad Discussion Guide*

Process

1. Explain the purpose of the activity. Set the stage by suggesting that the participants have fun with the activity.
2. Explain that you are asking each person to create two personal ads for themselves—similar to ads they have seen in magazines—except these ads should focus on meeting a teammate.
3. Distribute the handouts. Explain that in creating their ads, participants are to use the descriptors in the handout. Participants should select one descriptor from each column for a total of four words. Refer to the *Sample Personal Ad*. In the first ad, they are seeking a person with a similar profile. In the second, they are looking for a person with a different profile. In the second profile, the "seeks" is changed to "dissimilar" and the "goal" is changed to "mutual learning." Allow 10 to 15 minutes to select the words and create the poster. The posters should be "worn," i.e., pinned to the person or around the neck with string.
4. Refer to the *Personal Ad Discussion Guide* and ask people to begin Round 1 by walking around to find a person with a similar profile. The partners should move their chairs to a place where they can have a private conversation using the questions in the *Guide*. Allow 10 minutes.
5. Begin Round 2 by asking people to find a dissimilar person (with 3 or 4 different descriptors). Once again, ask that the partners move to a quiet place and begin their conversation using the Round 2 questions. Allow 10 minutes.
6. Begin Round 3 by asking people to form teams of six, with the goal of creating a diverse team (people with different descriptors in their profile). When the teams are formed, they should move to a private location and begin the conversation using the Round 3 suggestions.
7. Conclude the exercise with a debriefing, or give the teams a group problem or exercise to complete using their norms.

Debriefing

- What do you see as the purpose of this activity?
- What did you learn from the experience?
- What does this exercise tell us about team effectiveness?

- What are some of the advantages of a diversity of styles on a team?
- In your organization, to what extent are teams composed of a diverse set of people?
- Why is there a tendency for teams to be composed of like-minded people?
- What can be done to ensure a diverse team membership?

Variations

1. Change the words in the list of descriptors to words that more closely reflect the purpose of your workshop or meeting.
2. Other icebreakers are Activity 18: It's a Puzzlement: A Get-Acquainted Icebreaker; Activity 11: Forming New Teams: A Get-Acquainted and Introductory Activity; and Activity 50: Yea, Team! A Large-Group Icebreaker.

Worksheet — *Personal Ad: Descriptors*

Instructions: Please select one descriptor from each column to form a four-word description of yourself.

Column 1	Column 2	Column 3	Column 4
Dependable	Cooperative	Fun-loving	Facilitator
Assertive	Disciplined	Aggressive	Challenger
Focused	Supportive	Organized	Visionary
Practical	Humorous	Hands-on	Innovator
Demanding	Laid-back	Carefree	Listener
Candid	Daring	Confident	Hard worker
Careful	Trusting	Open-minded	Problem-solver

Worksheet

Sample Personal Ad

Personal Ad

Dependable

Cooperative

Fun-Loving

Facilitator

Seeks: Like-Minded Teammate

Goal: Positive Reinforcement

Personal Ad

Dependable

Cooperative

Fun-Loving

Facilitator

Seeks: Dissimilar Teammate

Goal: Mutual Learning

Worksheet

Personal Ad Discussion Guide

Instructions: Use the following questions to guide your meetings with your partner(s) in each round.

Round 1: Team Up with a Like-Minded Teammate (A Similar Profile).

- What do we have in common?
- What did you mean by _____ (select words in ad, such as *dependable*)?
- What are the positive aspects of our profile?
- What are the potential disadvantages?
- What are the positive outcomes of us teaming up?
- What are the potential disadvantages?

Round 2: Team Up with Someone with a Different Profile.

- Why did you select me?
- What strengths do we bring to each other?
- What are the potential disadvantages of us working together?
- What can we learn from each other?
- Would you rather team up with me, or with the person from Round 1?

Round 3: Form a Team of Six People, with the Goal of Creating a Diverse Group of People.

- Share your individual profiles and discuss what strengths you each bring to the team.
- Share what you need from each other to be a successful team.
- Develop a set of norms for this team, drawing on your individual profiles.

Activity 22

Project Rescue

Purpose

1. To explore the dynamics of problem-solving and decision-making
2. To become aware of team planning and role clarification
3. To become aware of cross-functional interdependencies

Group Size

Designed for a team-training workshop, with the participants divided into groups of five people each. The total number of participants is limited only by the space available and the ability of the facilitator to handle large groups.

Time

1 to 2 hours

Physical Setting

A room large enough for the groups to work comfortably with round or rectangular tables with chairs

Materials

1. Easel, flipcharts, markers, and masking tape or push pins for each team
2. A copy of *Background Sheet* for each team member
3. A copy of *Role Sheets* for each participant

143

Process

1. The facilitator gives a short talk on the need for collaboration and open communications to ensure overall team effectiveness. Further, the facilitator briefs the group on the concept of team formation and the need to clarify roles and establish team norms.
2. The facilitator forms groups of five, explains the activity, and gives each participant a role sheet, indicating that team members should not share their role sheet information sets with one another until after the activity has been completed.
3. The facilitator begins the activity and then monitors each team's progress and process.
4. After 60 minutes, the facilitator concludes the activity by asking each group to describe their work, and then leads a discussion on role conflict, team problem-solving, and team decision-making.

Debriefing

- What insights can we take away from this activity regarding our team?
- Is the problem-solving model presented a useful one for the purpose of our team?
- How can we apply the learnings from this activity to our team's efforts?

Variations

1. Change the *Role Sheets* to include typical roles on your teams.
2. Revise the case description to reflect current issues in your organization.
3. Try the related activity—Activity 41: The Product Development Team: A Simulation.

Worksheet

Background Sheet

You are an employee of DGI, Inc., a company that has been in business for nearly fifty years. DGI manufactures sandpaper (as well as other products). It is located in the city of Lytdeville. Because of the nature of the product, serious questions have been raised about the company's ability to compete in a global economy. The president of the company has asked a group of people to come together to develop a strategy to ensure the company's long-term success.

You have been asked to join this group. The group's first meeting is today.

Worksheet

Role Sheets

Note to Facilitator: Photocopy this page and then cut into five individual Role Sheets.

Role Sheet 1: The Sales Rep

You have been appointed to serve on the task force representing sales and marketing. Your goal is to take control of the team, using a power mode to influence what you believe the current market demands to be.

Role Sheet 2: The Product-Development Rep

You have been appointed to serve on the task team representing research and development. Your goal is to keep the company in the same product line, because you believe it to be correct.

Role Sheet 3: The Manufacturing Rep

You have been appointed to serve on the task team representing the manufacturing unit. Your goal is to maintain the status quo from a product standpoint, but you believe that expansion of the manufacturing operation to Europe is the best way to go global.

Role Sheet 4: The Finance Rep

You have been appointed the finance representative. Your goal is to reduce inventory levels, and you will fight any effort to redirect the company if you believe the move to be prohibitive from the standpoint of expense.

Role Sheet 5: The HR Rep

You have been asked to join the team to ensure that the human aspects of the future are considered.

Activity 23

Really . . . but I Thought

Purpose

1. To clarify expectations and conceptions of team members
2. To renegotiate roles within and among a work team
3. To create an awareness of the need for personal contracting

---

Group Size

A minimum of twelve members of an intact team

Time

2 hours

Physical Setting

A large room with wall space for posting flipchart pages, and chairs in a circle or around a conference table

---

Materials

1. Easel, flipchart, markers, and masking tape or push pins
2. A writing pad for each team member

Process

1. The team leader or facilitator gives a brief presentation on the four characteristics of *role* as defined by Gordon Allport:

   • Role expectations —What others expect of us
   • Role conception —What you see your role to be
   • Role acceptance —How we accept our role
   • Role behavior   —How we actually behave

2. The facilitator asks team members to evaluate each participant on the four elements, using the writing pad and working privately. Allow 30 minutes.
3. The team members also rate themselves on each characteristic.
4. The facilitator then asks the members to pair off randomly and share their work with their partner. Team members then find a new partner and again share their work. This activity should continue until each team member has had a one-on-one meeting with every other team member.
5. The facilitator gives a brief presentation on personal contracting and asks team members to make new contracts with each other.
6. The team concludes the activity by setting a time and date to review progress.

Debriefing

• What impact do you feel this activity will have on the future effectiveness of the team?
• How did each of you feel about having to evaluate each other?
• Do you each believe that you engaged in the process openly and honestly?
• How will each of you behave in the future as a result of this activity?

Variations

1. Step 2 can be done as prework.
2. The private negotiating sessions can be done in a group forum.

Activity 24

Refreshing the Team

Taking Stock of Where We Have Been and What We Need to Do to Move Ahead

Purpose

1. To allow members of an intact team to reflect on issues that might be blocking progress
2. To let go of old issues so the team can move forward

Group Size

Works best with groups of no more than ten members who have been together for more than six months

Time

90 minutes

Physical Setting

A space large enough for the group to work comfortably and without interruption. There should be enough wall space to hang a flipchart for each team member.

Materials

1. Easel, flipcharts, markers, and masking tape or push pins
2. Writing paper and pens or pencils

3. A copy of the *Team-Hindrance Issue Action Planning Guide* for each team member

Process

1. The facilitator introduces the activity by explaining that the purpose is to review the recent history of the team and to deal with issues that might be hindering its progress.
2. Group members are then asked to think of issues that they believe are hindering the progress of the group. They are then asked to list the elements of the issue on a sheet of writing paper, but not to share it with anyone. The purpose of this step is to help the team members collect their thoughts and organize the elements associated with their issue. Allow 5 minutes for this task.
3. They are then asked to draw a picture (using no words) representing their issue, and to be sure that all the elements are included somehow in their picture. Allow 15 minutes for this task.
4. Team members post their pictures on the wall. Then they walk around the room to view the pictures. Allow 5 minutes for this task.
5. Ask each member in turn to identify their drawing—to go to it and then explain it to the larger group. Allow 20 minutes for this step.
6. Facilitate a discussion geared to identifying a common list of "hindering" issues that emerge from the pictures. Post the list on the flipchart.
7. Form subgroups to address each of the issues. Ask each subgroup to develop an action plan to mitigate the issue. Use the *Team-Hindrance Issue Action Planning Guide.*
8. Each subgroup presents its action plan.
9. The facilitator then summarizes and debriefs the activity.

Debriefing

- How did you approach this activity?
- How did you feel about reflecting on the issue that was blocking your progress?
- How did the pictures help you to understand the issue?
- How do you think this activity will help you deal with the issue?
- How will the team as a whole benefit from this activity?

Variation

Other related activities include Activity 27: Roadblocks: A Constraint Activity and Activity 43: The Way We Are, and Want to Be: A Visioning Activity for an Intact Team.

Team-Hindrance Issue Action Planning Guide

1. Describe the hindrances in some detail.

_____

_____

_____

_____

2. What causes the hindrances to exist or continue?

_____

_____

_____

_____

3. What can be done to mitigate the hindrances?

_____

_____

_____

_____

4. Develop a list of steps to implement the solutions described in number 3. Indicate what needs to be done and who will do it.

_____

_____

_____

_____

Activity 25

R E S P E C T

*An Assessment Instrument**

Purpose

1. To increase capability to act in a respectful manner toward teammates
2. To gain insight into strengths and weaknesses in giving respect
3. To increase understanding of respectful behavior
4. To improve interpersonal relations among team members

Group Size

Effective with small teams or groups of four to six people. Larger groups can be divided into subgroups of the same number.

Time

1¹/₂ to 2 hours

Physical Setting

Chairs arranged in a circle or around a round or rectangular table

*This activity draws heavily on Sara Lawrence-Lightfoot's *Respect: An Exploration,* published by Perseus Books, 1999.

Materials

1. A copy of *R E S P E C T: A Self-Assessment Instrument* for each person
2. A copy of *R E S P E C T : Scoring Summary* for each person
3. A copy of *R E S P E C T: Action Planning Guide* for each person
4. A copy of *R E S P E C T: Feedback Survey* (optional) for each person

Process

1. Explain that the purpose of the *R E S P E C T: A Self-Assessment Instrument* is to gain an understanding of respect in teams as well as to increase your ability to act in a respectful manner toward your teammates.
2. Distribute a copy of the *R E S P E C T: A Self-Assessment Instrument*. Ask each person to complete it. When everyone is done, distribute the *R E S P E C T: Scoring Summary* handout. Ask everyone to score the instrument and review the interpretation of their results.
3. Present a lecture on the six areas incorporating the information from the *R E S P E C T: Scoring Summary* handout. Use *Respect: An Exploration* by Sara Lawrence-Lightfoot as a resource.
4. Create subgroups of two or three members to share their results. Get additional feedback, and discuss possible improvement actions. Allow 30 minutes.
5. Ask each person to create a personal action plan designed to increase their ability to be more respectful toward teammates and others. Allow 20 minutes.
6. Reconvene the subgroups and ask participants to share their action plans. Subgroup members provide feedback on the plan.
7. If time permits, team members can present their plans to the whole team.
8. Debrief the exercise based on the questions provided.

Debriefing

- What did you learn from this experience?
- How will this help you in the future?
- How will the team gain from this experience?
- What norms should the team add as a result of this experience?
- How differently do your teammates see you? (Using this question assumes you did not use the feedback version covered in Variation 2 below.)
- Among all the respectful behaviors, which ones are the most difficult

for you to practice on a regular basis? Which ones are the easiest for you? Why?

- Among all the negative respectful behaviors, which ones bother you the most when someone does it to you? Why?
- Why is respect so important for effective teamwork? How does a lack of respect help to break down teamwork?
- What impact does culture (corporate, ethnic, national) have on respect? What are some examples of behavior considered disrespectful in one culture that would be perfectly acceptable in another culture?

Variations

1. Ask people to complete and score the *R E S P E C T: A Self-Assessment Instrument* as a pre-work assignment prior to the meeting. If the instruments are submitted in advance, you can create a team profile and present it at the meeting.
2. Use the *R E S P E C T: Feedback Survey.* Prior to the meeting, ask each person to give the *R E S P E C T: Feedback Survey* to their teammates (at least five teammates). Then each person completes the self-assessment and submits it along with the feedback surveys to you. You prepare individual reports that include team members' scores and the scores of their teammates.

RESPECT: A Self-Assessment Instrument

Instructions: Please review each of the behaviors listed below and circle one number to indicate the extent to which you perceive yourself using these behaviors in your interactions with your teammates and others.

In my interactions with other people, I . . .	ALMOST NEVER	RARELY	SOMETIMES	FREQUENTLY	ALMOST ALWAYS
1. Encourage others to act independently.	1	2	3	4	5
2. Am open to questions about my decisions.	1	2	3	4	5
3. Treat others in a courteous manner.	1	2	3	4	5
4. Listen carefully to what other people say.	1	2	3	4	5
5. Honor their contributions.	1	2	3	4	5
6. Attempt to get in touch with their feelings.	1	2	3	4	5
7. Help them be in charge of their situation.	1	2	3	4	5
8. Am open to feedback about my behavior.	1	2	3	4	5
9. Am patient with those who may not fully understand the situation.	1	2	3	4	5
10. Give my full and undivided attention.	1	2	3	4	5
11. Treat other people as peers.	1	2	3	4	5
12. Try to see the world through their eyes.	1	2	3	4	5
13. Enable others to function with minimal supervision.	1	2	3	4	5
14. Willingly respond to concerns about my work.	1	2	3	4	5
15. Do not tolerate disrespectful behavior.	1	2	3	4	5
16. Am totally engrossed in what they are saying.	1	2	3	4	5

In my interactions with other people, I . . .	ALMOST NEVER	RARELY	SOMETIMES	FREQUENTLY	ALMOST ALWAYS
17. Try to know people as individuals.	1	2	3	4	5
18. Try to be nonjudgmental.	1	2	3	4	5
19. Give people the opportunity to participate in decisions that affect them.	1	2	3	4	5
20. Willingly change my point of view in the face of reasoned arguments.	1	2	3	4	5
21. Do not use derogatory language to characterize the ideas of other people.	1	2	3	4	5
22. Am fully present in the moment.	1	2	3	4	5
23. Find what is right in what other people say.	1	2	3	4	5
24. Am compassionate.	1	2	3	4	5
25. Encourage others to make their own choices.	1	2	3	4	5
26. Provoke dialogue and debate about my ideas.	1	2	3	4	5
27. Do not "look down" on others who might be different or think differently than me.	1	2	3	4	5
28. Am fully available when others need me.	1	2	3	4	5
29. Appreciate and acknowledge other people's efforts.	1	2	3	4	5
30. Try to understand the values and culture of other people.	1	2	3	4	5

RESPECT
Scoring Summary

Instructions: Please transfer your responses to the appropriate spaces and total each column. Then total the columns to obtain your overall R E S P E C T score.

Empowering	Openness and Empathy	Civility	Being "Present"	Valuing
1. _____	2. _____	3. _____	4. _____	5. _____
6. _____	7. _____	8. _____	9. _____	10. _____
11. _____	12. _____	13. _____	14. _____	15. _____
16. _____	17. _____	18. _____	19. _____	20. _____
21. _____	22. _____	23. _____	24. _____	25. _____
26. _____	27. _____	28. _____	29. _____	30. _____
Totals				
_____	_____	_____	_____	_____

Overall R E S P E C T Score = _____

Empowering

People who give respect empower others to act independently. They do not control the actions of others; rather, they free them by enabling them to do their best. Respectful people are also participative; they involve people in decisions that impact them. A score of 18 to 25 indicates an empowering person.

Openness and Empathy

Respectful people are open people. They respect the other person's ideas, opinions, and experiences. They willingly respond to questions about their own decisions, behaviors, and ideas. A score of 18 to 25 demonstrates an openness associated with giving respect.

Empathy implies that you respect others to the extent that you are willing to "walk a mile in their shoes." You gain insight into their view of the world and act in a compassionate and nonjudgmental fashion toward them. A score of 18 to 25 is indicative of a high degree of empathy.

Civility

To respect others you must treat them in a civil manner. You do not "talk down" or use derogatory language in your interactions with others. Respectful people are courteous and patient. If you scored between 18 and 25, you are a civil person.

Being "Present"

Respectful people are "there" for others. They concentrate and listen to what others are saying. They respect others by not drifting off, but rather by focusing on and responding to the other person. A score of 18 to 25 indicates you are "present" in your interactions with other people.

Valuing

When you respect others, you demonstrate that you value them as people. You acknowledge their contributions, treat them as peers, and care about them as individuals. If your score is between 18 and 25, you respect people by valuing them.

RESPECT
Action Planning Guide

1. Currently, I am respectful to my teammates and others in the following ways:

   _____

   _____

   _____

   _____

   _____

   _____

2. Currently, I am disrespectful to my teammates and others in the following ways:

   _____

   _____

   _____

   _____

   _____

3. Steps I will take to be more respectful to my teammates and others include:

   _____

   _____

   _____

   _____

   _____

RESPECT: Feedback Survey

Instructions: Please review each of the behaviors below and circle one number to indicate to what extent the person named in the blank space demonstrates the behavior.

Name: _____

During interactions with other people, this person . . .	ALMOST NEVER	RARELY	SOMETIMES	FREQUENTLY	ALMOST ALWAYS
1. Encourages others to act independently.	1	2	3	4	5
2. Is open to questions about decisions.	1	2	3	4	5
3. Treats others in a courteous manner.	1	2	3	4	5
4. Listens carefully to what other people say.	1	2	3	4	5
5. Honors their contributions.	1	2	3	4	5
6. Attempts to get in touch with their feelings.	1	2	3	4	5
7. Helps them be in charge of their situation.	1	2	3	4	5
8. Is open to feedback about behavior.	1	2	3	4	5
9. Is patient with those who may not fully understand the situation.	1	2	3	4	5
10. Gives them full and undivided attention.	1	2	3	4	5
11. Treats other people as peers.	1	2	3	4	5
12. Tries to see the world through their eyes.	1	2	3	4	5
13. Enables others to function with minimal supervision.	1	2	3	4	5
14. Willingly responds to concerns about work.	1	2	3	4	5
15. Does not tolerate disrespectful behavior.	1	2	3	4	5

Name: _____

During interactions with other people, this person . . .	ALMOST NEVER	RARELY	SOMETIMES	FREQUENTLY	ALMOST ALWAYS
16. Is totally engrossed in what others are saying.	1	2	3	4	5
17. Tries to know people as individuals.	1	2	3	4	5
18. Tries to be nonjudgmental.	1	2	3	4	5
19. Gives people the opportunity to participate in decisions that affect them.	1	2	3	4	5
20. Willingly changes point of view in the face of reasoned arguments.	1	2	3	4	5
21. Does not use derogatory language to characterize the ideas of other people.	1	2	3	4	5
22. Is fully present in the moment.	1	2	3	4	5
23. Finds what is right in what other people are saying.	1	2	3	4	5
24. Is compassionate.	1	2	3	4	5
25. Encourages others to make their own choices.	1	2	3	4	5
26. Provokes dialogue and debate about their ideas.	1	2	3	4	5
27. Does not "look down" on others who might be different or think differently.	1	2	3	4	5
28. Is fully available when needed.	1	2	3	4	5
29. Appreciates and acknowledges other people's efforts.	1	2	3	4	5
30. Tries to understand the values and culture of other people.	1	2	3	4	5

Activity 26

Rhyme Time

A Game That Teaches Team Concepts

Purpose

1. To introduce basic team concepts to a new group of team members
2. To provide an opportunity to work together on a team task
3. To examine the advantages and disadvantages of competition and collaboration between groups

---

Group Size

This activity works best with a group of five to seven members. If the group is larger, create subgroups that do the activity simultaneously.

Time

45 minutes to 1 hour

Physical Setting

Chairs in a circle or placed around a small conference table. If several subgroups are necessary, clusters of chairs should be placed around the room in such a way that each subgroup can have a private discussion.

Materials

1. A deck of cards containing the question. Photocopy the *Rhyme Time Questions* on card stock and then cut each page into individual cards. Put the deck into an envelope. Create a deck for each subgroup.
2. A copy of the *Rhyme Time Game Instructions* for each participant
3. A copy of the *Rhyme Time Answers* for each participant
4. A flipchart, markers, and masking tape or push pins

Process

1. Open the session by explaining that this activity is a fun way to learn some basic team concepts and tools that will be explored in depth later in the program.
2. Form subgroups of five to seven participants.
3. Give each person a copy of the game instructions.
4. Distribute an envelope containing the deck of cards to each subgroup.
5. Review the instructions with the team, including the sample questions. Ask each subgroup to try to come up with a rhyme for each example without looking at the answers. (You may want to cut off the bottom of the instructions containing the sample answers before you print your copies. You can then distribute the answers after the subgroups have completed the practice round).
6. Instruct the subgroups to begin the game. Allow 30 or 45 minutes to answer the questions.
7. Debrief the activity using the questions provided. Post relevant responses on the flipchart.

Debriefing

You can debrief the activity in two ways.

First, you can focus on how the groups worked on the task using some of the following questions:

- How did your group go about completing the task?
- What did your subgroup do that was especially helpful?
- What things hindered your ability to complete this task?
- Did you consider collaborating with the other subgroups in any way? (Note: You were not prohibited from working together with the other subgroups).

- If you did not work collaboratively with the other subgroups, why didn't you?
- If you were to do this activity again, what would you do differently?
- What did you learn about teamwork?
- How will you apply these learnings in your work environment?

Second, you can spend some time probing for understanding of the teamwork concepts highlighted in the game with questions such as:

- What is a *norm*? How do norms help a team?
- What is *brainstorming*? What are the rules of brainstorming?
- *Storming* is a stage of team development. What happens typically during this stage? What are the other stages? What happens during these other stages?
- What is the *Pareto Principle*? What is a Pareto Chart?
- What is the *Nominal Group Technique*? When is it useful?
- What is a *cause and effect diagram*?
- What is *consensus*? When is it best to use the consensus method? When should it be avoided?

Variation

If your time is limited, reduce the number of Rhyme Time questions. In addition, enforce a strict limit on the time available to answer the questions.

Rhyme Time Questions

What is a team rule that tells members how to behave during conflict?

What is a routine administrative task?

What is a successful group?

What is a hidden agenda?

What is a clear, unemotional point of view?

What is a project team review?

What is a meaningless use of a popular team decision-making method?

What is an exercise that results in a torrent of ideas?

Worksheet

Rhyme Time Questions (cont.)

What is a very successful use of a group brainstorming exercise?

What is an award given to a group of highly skilled people?

What term describes the beliefs of an 18th-century economist whose chart many teams use?

What is an ironic acknowledgment a team can give a manager who shows little interest in them?

What is a cause-and-effect diagram prepared by a team composed of well-to-do members?

What is an informal recognition given as a natural part of the regular work day?

What is a group action plan?

Rhyme Time
Game Instructions

Flow of the Game

Your group will receive an envelope containing a deck of cards. On each card is a question pertaining to a team concept, idea, or tool. Begin the game by pulling a card out of the envelope and reading the question.

Your team task is to come up with a pair of *rhyming words* that answers the question. As a team, your goal is to answer as many questions as possible during the time allocated.

Samples

Here are a few examples. Try to guess the two rhyming words that answer these questions. Spend some time working on your answers before you check the sample answers below.

What is a boring seabird?

What do you get from the best grapes?

What is an excellent detail?

Rules

There are no rules. Each subgroup has been given a deck of cards with the same questions. You may organize your team in any way that makes sense in order to complete the task . . . to answer as many questions as possible using pairs of rhyming words.

Sample Answers

A boring seabird is a DULL GULL.

The best grapes give you FINE WINE.

An excellent detail is a TERRIFIC SPECIFIC.

Worksheet

Rhyme Time
Answers

Rhyme	*Question*
Storm Norm	What is a Team Rule that tells members how to behave during conflict?
Clerk Work	What is a routine administrative task?
Kean Team	What is a successful group?
Mole Goal	What is a hidden agenda?
Objective Perspective	What is a clear, unemotional point of view?
Direction Inspection	What is a project team review?
Consensus Nonsensus	What is a meaningless use of a popular team decision-making method?
Brainstorm Rainstorm	What is an exercise that results in a torrent of ideas?
Phenomenal Nominal	What is a very successful use of a group brainstorming exercise?
Technician Recognition	What is an award given to a group of highly skilled people?
Pareto Credo	What term describes the beliefs of an 18-century economist whose chart many teams use?
Bored Award	What is an ironic acknowledgment a team can give a manager who shows little interest in them?
Hightone Fishbone	What is a cause-and-effect diagram prepared by a team composed of well-to-do members?
Herbal Verbal	What is an informal recognition given as a natural part of the regular work day?
Team Scheme	What is a group action plan?

ctivity 27

Roadblocks

A Constraint Activity

Purpose

To become aware of the various roadblocks that can constrain team effectiveness

Group Size

Fifteen to thirty people in a team-training workshop

Time

1 hour

Physical Setting

A room large enough for the entire group, as well as breakout rooms for subgroups

Materials

1. Easel, flipchart, and markers for each group
2. A copy of the *Leader Instruction Sheet* for each group
3. Role descriptions for each team leader. Each role description can be printed

on a 3 × 5 index card or photocopied and cut into three sheets. See the *Role Description Sheet.*

4. A copy of the *Situation Worksheet* for each participant
5. A copy of the *Observer's Worksheet* for each group

Process

1. The facilitator gives a brief talk on how roadblocks can prevent a team from reaching its goals and objectives.
2. The facilitator explains the purpose of the activity and the agenda.
3. The facilitator selects three people to serve as team leaders. The team leaders are given one copy of the *Leader Instruction Sheet* each, one *Role Description Sheet*, and a *Situation Worksheet*. The team leaders then go off for 5 minutes to review the handouts.
4. The facilitator selects three participants, one per group, to be observers and reviews the *Observer's Worksheet* with them.
5. The facilitator assigns the remaining participants to teams and gives each person a copy of the *Situation Worksheet.*
6. The team leaders return and begin the activity.
7. After 20 minutes, the activity is ended. The observers provide feedback and discuss the impact of the leader's behavior on the team.
8. The teams reassemble to discuss roadblocks and which processes they used to deal with them.

Debriefing

- Describe what happened during the activity.
- Describe the interactions among and between members.
- What are the key learning points for the team?
- How will you apply them in the future with your group?

Variations

1. A work team issue can be used as the basis for the activity.
2. Other related activities include Activity 24: Refreshing the Team: Taking Stock of Where We Have Been and What We Need to Do to Move Ahead and Activity 43: The Way We Are, and Want to Be: A Visioning Activity for an Intact Team.

Worksheet — *Leader Instruction Sheet*

1. Read your role description. Learn your role. Feel free to add ideas and opinions as long as they are consistent with your basic role.

2. Don't reveal your role description to anyone. Stay in your role for the duration of the exercise.

3. Don't overact.

Worksheet

Role Description Sheet

Note to facilitator: Photocopy this page and then cut into three separate Leader Role Sheets.

Roadblocks Leader Role 1

- You expect well-developed solutions that are practical and logical, and that are a credit to you and your ability to manage the team.
- You want to achieve consensus.

Roadblocks Leader Role 2

- You don't really want a solution, and will stall as long as possible.
- You can use "E-commerce won't work in our industry," "It will cost too much," and other similar idea-killers to block the team.
- Your intent is to reject suggestions.

Roadblocks Leader Role 3

- You have a preconceived solution.
- You consider any suggestion a weakening of your idea. Therefore, minimize other ideas unless they can enhance your idea.
- You don't want the group to know you have a preselected solution.

Situation Worksheet

There is a movement in the company to open an e-commerce unit in a city located fifty miles from the company headquarters. A number of issues have been raised by various groups—employees, townspeople, stockholders, and public officials. Some of these issues include:

1. Who will staff the new facility?
2. What will happen to the traditional business at the company headquarters?
3. How will the new facility be managed and operated?

Your team has been asked to develop and present ideas on how to identify and solve the problems related to this new venture.

Observer's Worksheet

1. How would you describe the leader's behavior during the meeting?

   _____

   _____

   _____

   _____

2. What impact did the leader's behavior have on the group?

   _____

   _____

   _____

   _____

3. How far did the team get in reaching its objective?

   _____

   _____

   _____

   _____

4. How could the team have been more successful?

   _____

   _____

   _____

   _____

Activity 28

Selecting a Problem Solution

Purpose

1. To teach a team or team leaders the factors that should be considered in selecting the best solution to a problem
2. To teach a team or team leaders a process for deciding among various alternative solutions to a problem

Group Size

Works best with an intact team of four to twelve people or in a team-training workshop of up to twenty people

Time

1 to 2 hours

Physical Setting

With an intact team, a table and chairs.
In a training workshop, groups of tables and chairs spread out around the room.

Materials

1. A copy of the *Ratings Scales* for each person
2. A copy of the *Solution Worksheet* for each person

3. A copy of the *Action Plan Worksheet* for each person
4. Easel, flipchart, and markers

Process

1. This activity takes place after a team has generated several solutions to a problem.
2. Distribute a copy of the *Solution Worksheet* to each person. Tell the team to write a brief description of each solution in the left column of the worksheet. If necessary, explain what is meant by each of the factors across the top of the worksheet. Special attention should be given to types of typical costs (labor, materials) and benefits (cost reduction, quality improvement).
3. Post the totals for each solution on a flipchart. Lead a discussion on each of the solutions by focusing on the relative importance of the factors.
4. Move the discussion toward a consensus on one solution.
5. If time permits, develop an action plan using the handout provided.
6. Debrief the activity using the questions provided.

Debriefing

- How do you feel about the process by which the team decided on a solution?
- How helpful was the solution worksheet?
- What would have improved the process?
- How committed do you feel the team is to the solution selected?
- How would you approach the task of selecting a solution in the future?

Variations

1. Each person completes the worksheet prior to the session.
2. In a team session, case materials using a simulated problem and possible solutions can be created for this exercise.

Rating Scales

Instructions

1. Prior to rating the solutions, discuss the categories as they relate to the problems to make sure that everyone is clear about their meaning.
2. List the solutions in the column to the left. It is assumed that they all adequately solve the problem.
3. Using the above scales, rate each problem in the five categories and compute the total.
4. Develop a team score for each solution by sharing your individual ratings for each category and then computing a total. (It might be useful to post the ratings on a flipchart and then discuss the reasons for each.)
5. Circle the highest-rated solution and proceed to the preparation of an action plan.

Benefits	*Cost*	*Ease of Implementation*	*Time*	*Secondary Impacts*
1. The expected benefits will be minimal.	1. The cost will be very high.	1. It will be very difficult to implement.	1. It will be more than 6 months before benefits are seen.	1. It also results in some significant negative impacts.
2. The expected benefits will be good.	2. The cost will be high.	2. It will be difficult to implement.	2. It will be 3 to 6 months before benefits are seen.	2. It also results in some negative impacts.
3. The expected benefits will be very good.	3. The cost will be low.	3. There will be a few obstacles to putting it into practice.	3. It will be 1 to 3 months before benefits are seen.	3. It also results in additional positive impacts.
4. The expected benefits will be outstanding.	4. There will be no added cost.	4. It can be easily put into practice.	4. Benefits will be seen in fewer than 30 days.	4. It also results in some additional significant positive impacts.

Solution Worksheet

	Solution Description	Benefits	Costs	Ease of Implementation	Time	Secondary Impacts	Total
1							
2							
3							
4							
5							

Action Plan Worksheet

What Needs to Be Done?	Who Will Do It?	Completion Date

Activity 29

Separate Tables

Resolving Intergroup Conflict

Purpose

1. To help two teams identify the sources of their conflict
2. To help two teams develop a plan for resolving their conflict

Group Size

A team-building session for two teams. Works best with teams of no more than ten people each.

Time

2¹/₂ to 3 hours

Physical Setting

One large meeting room and one break-out room

Materials

Easel, flipchart, markers, and masking tape or push pins

Process

1. Explain the purpose of the activity. Set some positive norms for the session (e.g., listening, focusing on the issue).

2. Ask one group to move to the break-out room while the other one stays in the meeting room. Give each group a few sheets of flipchart paper, markers, and masking tape or push pins. Each team is to prepare a list of answers to the two questions that follow. Allow 20 to 30 minutes to complete this task.
   —What does the other team do that inhibits our ability to get our job done, or in general, just "bugs" us?
   —What do we do that inhibits the other team's ability to get its job done or in general "bugs" them?
3. The teams reassemble in the large room and post their flipcharts on the wall. Participants walk around and read the lists.
4. Team members are encouraged to ask questions for clarification of the items on the list.
5. The facilitator leads a discussion directed toward the identification of key issues standing in the way of effective intergroup teamwork. The most important issues are listed on the flipchart. If too many issues are listed, they should be ranked in order of importance.
6. The facilitator writes each issue on a separate sheet of flipchart paper and posts them on the wall around the room. Participants may work on the issue that interests them by moving to the area where the flipchart paper is posted. Teams are formed on this basis to develop action plans for addressing the issue. The only stipulations are that the teams include a reasonably equal number of people from each group, and that the team not be too large.
7. Teams are asked to come up with a problem statement, causes of the problem, and an action plan, including responsibilities and a timetable. Allow 30 to 45 minutes.
8. Each team prepares and presents a report on its plan. The other teams react.
9. The session concludes with a summary and debriefing by the facilitator and a review of next steps based on the action plans.

Debriefing

- How do you feel about this experience?
- To what extent did the real issues surface?
- How different would the results have been if the two groups developed their lists in the same room? With one group observing the other?
- Why does open communication require privacy and anonymity?
- To what extent will action plans increase trust, open communication, and reduce unproductive conflict?

- How would you change the activity to make it more effective?
- Can you see other applications for this exercise?
- What did you learn about such things as team decision-making, use of team resources, communication, and planning?
- If you were to do this activity again, what would you do differently?
- How important is a review of process in a project review? How can you incorporate a process review in your project in the future?

Variations

1. The facilitator meets with each team prior to the session and collects data on the relationships, using the same questions. The session begins with a summary of the comments. Pick up the activity at Step 4 above.
2. If more time is available in Step 2, ask each group to guess how the other group will answer the questions.

Skills for Sale

An Assessment Simulation

Purpose

1. To critically review the skills, capabilities, and potential of a team
2. To develop a strategy for marketing the services of a team
3. To explore a team's strengths and weaknesses

Group Size

This is a team-building activity designed for use with an intact work team of up to twelve people.

Time

3 hours

Physical Setting

Chairs arranged in a circle, or tables and chairs arranged in conference style

Materials

1. Easel, flipcharts, markers, and masking tape or push pins
2. Paper and pens for each team member

Process

1. The team leader tells the group to imagine they are a consulting group (consulting in the general area of their unit's expertise in an organization of any size). Further, they are told that because the economy is changing, major changes in business strategy will have to be made. In fact, the team leader's boss has made it clear that the team will have to respond to the demands of e-commerce as a profit center by creating a Web marketing approach and selling its services to outside organizations. The alternative is to shut down the department and lay off the staff. The team leader is given six months to launch the new unit.
2. The team leader then leads the group through an identification of their skills and determines which skills might be useful in the new business.
3. The team identifies its shortcomings and any additional skills that will be needed.
4. The team determines how the current skills can be enhanced and what additional skills can be acquired.
5. The team leader then reviews what has been learned during the activity, and lists action steps to be taken.
6. At the end of the session, the team leader and the members debrief the activity and build an action plan to implement the steps needed to enhance the team's overall base.

Debriefing

- How realistic is the impact of e-commerce and the Web on you and your team?
- Did this activity help focus the team on the development of alternative goals and action plans for your team?
- If yes . . . how will you move forward with your new plans?
- If no . . . why not, and what will your team do to take advantage of new approaches to business?

Variations

1. The assessment activity can be done in advance.
2. The team can obtain input from their current customers, based on their skills and capabilities. The input can also include ideas on what additional skills and capabilities the customers would like to see the team develop.

Activity 31

SOS

An OD Intervention

Purpose

1. To assess the degree to which your organization supports teamwork as a business strategy
2. To identify the supports required for the success of teamwork as a business strategy
3. To develop a plan for enhancing the organizational supports for teamwork as a business strategy

Group Size

Works best with a group of four to eight people

Time

6 hours (can be divided into two or three short sessions)

Physical Setting

A small room with a conference table and chairs

Materials

1. A copy of the *Survey of Organizational Supports (SOS)* for each person
2. An easel, flipchart, markers, and masking tape or push pins
3. A copy of the *Organizational Action Plan* for each participant

Process

1. Prior to the meeting, distribute the survey to a representative sample of employees in the organization. Summarize the results and prepare a report for use by the team leader.
2. At the meeting, isolate the key factors that need to be improved in order to increase support for teamwork. Discuss examples of the current supports and factors working against teamwork. You can use the flipchart to record and organize discussion input. Try to work on only a few issues at a time.
3. Develop an action plan for each of the issues. If appropriate, use the *Organizational Action Plan*.

Debriefing

- What conclusions can you draw from this activity?
- Do the results of the assessment lead you to believe that teamwork is an integral part of your business strategy?
- What supports are in place to foster the success of teamwork in your organization?
- What can you do to enhance the organization's support for teamwork?

Variations

1. Revise the *SOS* to include factors that are more closely related to your organization.
2. Revise the *SOS* to include a space for respondents to write in examples of the supports (e.g., preparing an agenda, dealing with conflict).
3. Another assessment instrument is Activity 13: Got Culture? A Team-Assessment Tool.

Survey of Organizational Supports (SOS)

Instructions: Please indicate the degree to which you agree or disagree with the following statements. Circle one number.

Statements	STRONGLY DISAGREE	DISAGREE	NEITHER AGREE NOR DISAGREE	AGREE	STRONGLY AGREE
1. Our vision/values/mission statement includes teamwork as a key business strategy.	1	2	3	4	5
2. Teamwork is a prominent part of all statements, presentations, and reports by our organization.	1	2	3	4	5
3. The management team of our organization encourages everyone to work as a team.	1	2	3	4	5
4. Promotions, key assignments, and projects go to people who are positive team players.	1	2	3	4	5
5. The performance-appraisal system incorporates team-player behaviors as important factors in assessing employee performance.	1	2	3	4	5
6. Individual performance on cross-functional teams is included in the performance appraisal prepared by the functional department manager.	1	2	3	4	5
7. The formal awards program acknowledges the contributions of team players and teams.	1	2	3	4	5
8. Informal, day-to-day recognition regularly acknowledges the contributions of team players and teams.	1	2	3	4	5

Statements	STRONGLY DISAGREE	DISAGREE	NEITHER AGREE NOR DISAGREE	AGREE	STRONGLY AGREE
9. The recruitment and hiring procedures support our efforts to increase the quantity and quality of team players in our organization.	1	2	3	4	5
10. The stories and myths that underline the norms in our organization demonstrate positive support for teamwork.	1	2	3	4	5
11. The formal work environment (space and equipment) makes it easy for teams to be successful.	1	2	3	4	5
12. The informal work environment is relaxed and casual, and it encourages spontaneous teamwork.	1	2	3	4	5
13. The organization's planning process requires the involvement of work teams in the development of plans.	1	2	3	4	5
14. Teams have an important place in the organization's formal structure.	1	2	3	4	5

Strengths (factors that support teamwork):

_____

_____

_____

_____

Areas for improvement (factors that need to be improved):

_____

_____

_____

_____

Organizational Action Plan

1. **Current reality.** Describe the organizational support that needs to be added, deleted, or strengthened.

   _____

   _____

   _____

   _____

2. **Desired future state.** Describe the organizational support you want and how you want it to function.

   _____

   _____

   _____

   _____

3. **Getting from here to there.** Describe how you plan to get from the current reality to the desired future state. Include what needs to be done, who will do it, and when it will be completed.

What	Who	When
_____	_____	_____
_____	_____	_____
_____	_____	_____
_____	_____	_____
_____	_____	_____

Activity 32

Team-Building Interview Guide

Purpose

1. To collect data on the strengths and weaknesses of the team
2. To collect data to plan a team-building intervention
3. To explain the team-building process to the participants

Group Size

The suggested format is individual interviews. Therefore, a maximum of fifteen people is recommended. Beyond this size, a written survey is the preferred data-gathering tool.

Time

30 minutes to 1 hour for each interview

Physical Setting

A private office or small meeting room

Materials

A copy of the *Team-Building Interview Guide* for each participant

Process

1. Begin the meeting by introducing yourself and describing your role as a team-building consultant. Explain the purpose of the interview, the format of the interview, what will happen to the data, who will see the data, and how it will be used in the team-building process. Make sure you stress the confidential nature of the interview.
2. Give the person a copy of the guide and explain that you will ask the questions and write the answers on your copy.
3. If you do not know the person, you might wish to begin by asking for a job description. Then move on to the questions on the *Team-Building Interview Guide*. Probe and follow up on answers as appropriate, especially changes that would make the team more effective.
4. At the end of the interview, go back over the guide and review your notes with the person. Ask if your notes are accurate. Review what will happen to the data and the next steps in the team-building process.
5. Thank the person.
6. Review your notes before the next interview and add any final thoughts.

Debriefing

- What new data did this activity uncover about the strengths and weaknesses of your team?
- What new data did this activity uncover about your contribution to the success of the team?
- What strategies will most efficiently minimize the weaknesses uncovered and maximize the strengths?

Variations

1. If conditions do not allow for individual interviews, use the *Team-Building Interview Guide* to conduct a series of small-group interviews. Record the answers on flipchart paper.
2. Add or delete questions to tailor the guide to your specific team. For example, with a new team you might want to ask whether people have concerns about being on a new team. With a cross-functional team you might want to ask about relationships with people from other parts of the company.
3. An alternative approach is to use a survey instrument. See Activity 3: Characteristics of an Effective Work Team: An Assessment Activity.

Worksheet

Team-Building Interview Guide

1. Briefly describe your team in terms of membership, structure, and purpose.

   _____

   _____

   _____

2. What are the key challenges facing your team now?

   _____

   _____

   _____

3. What do you see as the strengths of your team?

   _____

   _____

   _____

4. What areas need improvement?

   _____

   _____

   _____

5. What changes would make the team more effective? (What can the team do and what can the organization do to support the team.)

   _____

   _____

   _____

6. Are the roles clear? Is everyone clear about what is expected from them?

    _____

    _____

    _____

7. How would you describe team meetings? Are improvements needed?

    _____

    _____

    _____

8. How does your team handle internal conflict?

    _____

    _____

    _____

9. How does your team interact with other teams, clients, and key stakeholders in the organization?

    _____

    _____

    _____

10. What would make this team-building session successful for you? What would you like to see happen as a result of the session? What would you personally like to walk away with?

    _____

    _____

    _____

11. What else should I know that would help to make this event successful?

    _____

    _____

    _____

Activity 33

Team Conflict Mode

Purpose

1. To learn the five modes of dealing with conflict
2. To identify your team's dominant conflict mode
3. To improve your team's ability to use the collaborative mode

---

Group Size

Works best with an intact team of four to eight people. Can be adapted for use in a team-training workshop with a larger group.

Time

2 hours

Physical Setting

A small room with a conference table and chairs

Materials

1. A copy of *Conflict Management Mode* chart for each person
2. A copy of *Conflict Management Mode Definitions* for each person
3. An easel, flipchart, and markers

Process

1. Explain the purpose of the activity. Distribute the *Conflict Management Mode*. Review and explain each method of dealing with conflict. Ask the team for examples of each method.
2. Working individually, team members plot their perception of the team's dominant mode on the grid.
3. The leader draws a large copy of the grid on the flipchart. Participants place dots on the grid to indicate their perception of the team's conflict mode. The team discusses the various perceptions.
4. Debrief the activity.

Debriefing

• What insights have you gained from this activity?
• How can your team move its overall approach from its place to a more win/win position?

Variations

1. Team members can plot their personal conflict mode, present their perception to the group, and receive feedback from the rest of the team.
2. Two interdependent teams can meet and use the *Conflict Management Mode* to plot their perceptions of the other team's dominant mode.
3. For an exercise that focuses on individual conflict styles, see Activity 5: Communicating about Conflict: Learning Ways to Resolve Conflict.

Conflict Management Mode

High	Compete (Win/Lose)	Collaborate (Win/Win)
		Compromise
Low	Avoid (Lose/Lose)	Accommodate (Lose/Win)

Motivation to Resolve

Low   High

Trust

Conflict Management Mode Definitions

Compete

Go all out to win, be concerned about objectives only.

Compromise

Settle for "half a loaf."

Accommodate

Yield or subordinate one's own concerns to those of the other party.

Collaborate

Work toward mutual problem-solving, recognizing both parties' goals.

Avoid

Deny, suppress, or put aside the difference.

Activity 34

Team Development

A Grid Perspective

Purpose

1. To diagnose and evaluate the stage of development of an intact work team
2. To compare team development with performance independence
3. To compare team members' perceptions of team development at a given time

Group Size

A team of seven to twelve is best, but larger teams can be organized into subgroups as long as final grids are compared

Time

1 hour

Physical Setting

Tables and chairs arranged in conference style or a U-shape

Materials

1. Pencils or marking pens
2. A copy of the *Team-Development Grid* for each participant
3. Easel and flipchart

Process

1. The team leader gives a brief lecture on team development, stressing the notion of interdependence and the need to become self-directed. The team leader also discusses the process of self-renewal.
2. The team leader then quickly defines the following terms:
   a. interdependence (the interactions of members)
   b. self-direction (the level of team autonomy)
   c. self-renewal (the willingness to learn and grow)
3. The team leader asks each member to review the *Team-Development Grid,* explaining the self-direction axis and self-renewal axis. The team leader explains that in order to complete the team-development grid, participants plot their perception of the team's self-directedness and self-renewal. The team-development grid questionnaire will help them quantify where they stand. The team leader then locates the intersection of the scores they have assigned. For example, if they believe that the team is 75 percent self-directed and 50 percent self-renewing, they would place a mark in the upper left-hand quadrant of the grid.

Debriefing

- What is the impact of your score and the team scores on the ability of the team to be successful?
- What is the relationship between your scores and the team's performance?
- What actions will you and your team take to improve the scores?

Variation

The grid can be completed by team members prior to participating in the workshop.

Worksheet

Team-Development Grid

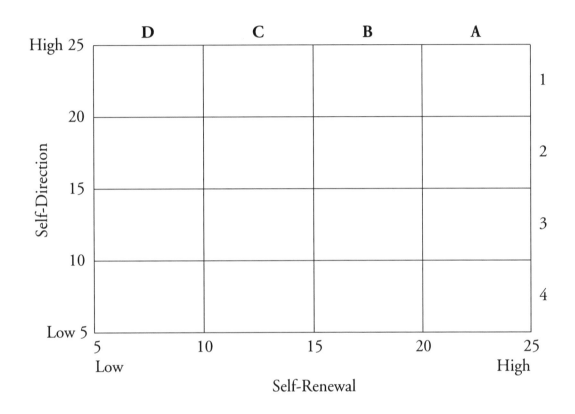

Worksheet

Team-Development Grid Questions to Establish the Degrees of Self-Direction and Self-Renewal

Self-Direction

	Agree		Neutral		Disagree
1. Our team is highly autonomous.	5	4	3	2	1
2. Our team is empowered to act independently.	5	4	3	2	1
3. Our team is empowered to make decisions.	5	4	3	2	1
4. Our team is able to act without seeking higher-level approval.	5	4	3	2	1
5. Our team is engaged in continuous improvement.	5	4	3	2	1

Self-Renewal

	Agree		Neutral		Disagree
1. Our team is fully prepared to achieve its goals.	5	4	3	2	1
2. Our team engages in continuous learning as a team.	5	4	3	2	1
3. Our team members respect each others' skills and talents.	5	4	3	2	1
4. Our team is able to secure the resources it needs to achieve its goals.	5	4	3	2	1
5. Our team strives to determine its current and future learning needs.	5	4	3	2	1

Activity 35

Teams That Change

Building a Team Plan for Change

Purpose

1. To help the team understand that in order for a team to change, it must see the benefit of change
2. To help the team see a new perspective

Group Size

An intact work group of any size that has been together for more than six months and that is faced with an uncertain future

Time

60 to 90 minutes (This activity might take more than one session.)

Physical Setting

A comfortable space, with enough wall space to post flipcharts of responses to various questions

Materials

Easel, flipcharts, markers, and masking tape or push pins

Process

1. The facilitator introduces the activity by pointing out that the best way for a team to change is to openly discuss and fully participate in the task so that members can see a new perspective.
2. The facilitator then begins the activity by asking participants to answer the following question:

    Why should we change?
3. Assist the group by first asking them to brainstorm items in the news that affect their team's ability to be successful. Post these responses on a flipchart. To stimulate the group's thinking, the facilitator might ask such questions as:

    What's happening to the competition?

    What do our customers really want?
4. Discuss these questions and answers. Seek agreement that change is required. Allow 20 minutes for this task.
5. Repeat the process above for the next question:

    What should we change?
6. Ask the team to brainstorm a list of things that need to change. Facilitate a discussion of the priority of the items, and develop a new strategic statement for the team.
7. Ask the group to compare this new statement with the existing strategy statement of the team looking for two or three main issues. These issues will become the agenda for change.
8. Having completed these steps, ask the team to determine what tasks need to be completed and by whom. The facilitator helps the team build an action plan to ensure a successful change effort.

Debriefing

- Did this exercise meet your expectations?
- Do each of you feel that this effort will help the team move forward? Why or why not?
- What needs to be done now?

Variations

1. Have the group come up with change action steps prior to the session.
2. Ask the group to collect data from other teams, departments, etc., prior to the session about their perceptions of what this team needs to change.

Activity 36

Tell-a-Story Teaming

An Exercise in Creativity and Productivity

Purpose

1. To help team members enhance their creative-thinking skills
2. To stimulate innovation in team work

Group Size

Works well with large groups, but requires at least eight members

---

Time

60 minutes

Physical Setting

Space large enough for several small groups to work comfortably

---

Materials

1. Index cards (5 × 7)
2. Pens and paper
3. Flipchart and markers

Process

1. Prepare sets of index cards by writing a category on each card. (See *Index Card Topics.*)
2. Facilitator begins by explaining that the purpose of the activity is to stimulate creative thinking and stronger team work.
3. The facilitator divides the group into subgroups and gives one set of index cards to each subgroup. The index cards are placed face-down so that the participants cannot see them.
4. Each team member selects a card and writes down an example of that topic.
5. The facilitator then instructs the subgroups to develop a short story that incorporates each of the group's topic examples. The facilitator should encourage the subgroups to use their imaginations and be as creative as possible.
6. After 30 minutes, reconvene the team and ask each subgroup to tell their story to the whole team.
7. Conclude the activity with a general debriefing.

Debriefing

- Did you find the activity helpful? Challenging?
- How did the activity proceed?
- How do you feel about your contribution? The contribution of others?
- Discuss the roles of each team member (leadership, followership, etc.).
- How will this activity help you back on the job as the team goes about its work?
- How might this activity be improved?

Variation

The facilitator assigns specific index cards to team members.

Worksheet   *Index Card Topics*

Prior to the activity, prepare several sets of index cards with the following topics, placing only one topic on each card:

Person	Activity
Place	Food
Object	Occupation
Animal	Mood

These eight cards are only suggestions. The facilitator should consider revising them, depending on the nature of the team's work.

Activity 37

The Car Case

Learning How to Define a Problem

Purpose

1. To teach quality teams and other problem-solving teams how to recognize a real problem
2. To teach quality teams and other problem-solving teams how to write a clear problem statement

---

Group Size

Works with an intact team of up to twelve people, or as a session in a team-training workshop. In a training workshop, the class can be divided into small groups.

Time

45 minutes to 1 hour

Physical Setting

Round or rectangular table and chairs

Materials

1. A copy of *The Car Case* for each person
2. Easel, flipchart, markers, and masking tape or push pins, or overhead projector, screen, several blank transparencies, and transparency pens

Process

1. Explain the purpose of the session. Ask team members to brainstorm answers to the question, "What is a problem?" Post definitions on a flipchart or overhead transparency.
2. Distribute *The Car Case*. Ask the team to read the case, decide what they think is the problem, and write a problem statement.
3. The facilitator leads a discussion on the various answers. The team develops a problem statement together and the facilitator writes it on the flipchart or overhead transparency. The statement is edited by the team. (Note: The problem is that the car won't start.)
4. Return to the original list of definitions and ask if there are any additions as a result of the exercise. Reduce and edit the list, with the goal of developing a clear definition of the problem.
5. Debrief the exercise, using the questions provided.

Debriefing

- What is the point of this exercise?
- Why is it important to have clearly defined the problem?
- What are some typical mistakes we make in defining problems?
- What did you learn from this activity?
- How will you apply these learnings to your team's situation?
- What will be some of the business benefits of having clear definitions of the problem?

Variations

1. Give a lecture on what is a problem and the elements of a good problem statement, before analyzing the case.
2. Before working on the case, give the team some sample problem statements to analyze in order to determine whether they meet the criteria of an acceptable problem statement.
3. A related activity is Activity 28: Selecting a Problem Solution.

Worksheet

The Car Case

Background Information

Your job requires you to be at work promptly at 7:00 A.M. to relieve the midnight shift operator. Driving by car, it takes 20 minutes to reach your job.

Your spouse also has a car and takes the children to school on the way to work (two days a week).

The children start school at 8:00 A.M. and your spouse begins work at 8:30 A.M. One of your children has a driver's license.

You have a neighbor two houses away who works where you do, but he begins work at 7:30 A.M., 30 minutes later than you do. He carpools with two other men. A bus that goes by the plant passes a block away from your house. However, the first bus in the morning does not get to the plant until 7:30 A.M.

The Situation

On Monday morning, you try to start the car at 6:35 A.M., as usual, and find that it will not start. It will turn over slowly, but will not start. You not only need the car to get to work, but you also need it to go out of town to a training session tomorrow morning. This is the third time this winter the car has not started.

1. What is the problem?

   _____

   _____

   _____

2. Write a problem statement.

   _____

   _____

   _____

Activity 38

The Case of the Free-Falling Team

Developing High-Performing Team Players

Purpose

1. To help team members analyze their strengths and weaknesses
2. To help the team members create personal action plans for growth

Group Size

Works well with teams of fewer than ten members

Time

1 hour

Physical Setting

Space large enough for the group to work comfortably and to post flipcharts on the walls

Materials

1. A copy of the case study for each team member
2. Easel, flipchart, markers, and masking tape or push pins

Process

1. The facilitator explains the purpose of the activity is to develop a problem-solving process that is related to personal growth and development as well as team development and growth.
2. The facilitator distributes the brief case study asking participants to read it and think about its implications. Allow 2 to 3 minutes for this task.
3. Form subgroups of three or four members each and ask them to act as if they were consultants hired by the team leader to solve this mystery. Have the group prepare a report, using the flipchart to record their findings. Allow 20 minutes for the case analysis task.
4. Reconvene the group and have them report their results.
5. The facilitator summarizes the activity by asking participants to relate problems and their solutions to the problems on their team.

Debriefing

- How did this activity help you to better understand your team and its issues?
- How does this activity help you develop personally as a team player?

Variations

1. The case study can be made specific to the work of the team.
2. Team members are asked to act as if they were colleagues, rather than consultants.

The Case of the Free-Falling Team

Worksheet

The team seems to be in free-fall. It has been intact for more than nine months, having started with team training. It was working well, but recently the members have fallen back into old behaviors. Some of the behaviors they engage in are:

- They are failing to share necessary information.
- They are writing and sending protective e-mails.
- They are doing only what they need to do individually.
- They are behaving badly in team meetings.

The team leader is aware that the team is free-falling but has little idea of what to do about it.

Activity 39

The Collaborative

Creating the Conditions for the Collaborative Team

Purpose

1. To clarify and expand the norms of a team's behavior
2. To provide the group with a framework to understand and live within their chosen norms
3. To gain an understanding of collaboration and the need for interdependence

Group Size

Unlimited, but the time will vary based on the size of the group

Time

45 to 90 minutes, depending on group size

Physical Setting

Any room with wall space for mounting flipchart pages

Materials

1. Flipcharts, markers, and masking tape or push pins
2. Self-stick removable notes
3. Index cards, 3 × 5

Process

1. Explain the purpose of the exercise, highlighting the role that collaboration plays in creating effective teams.
2. Discuss the concept of collaborative norms and the role they play in the team-development process.
3. Ask the participants to take sheets of flipchart paper and list one collaborative norm per sheet. Post them around the room.
4. Give out Post-it notes and ask participants to write how the norms will express themselves when they are practiced by the group. For example, willingness to share: People will be saying what they have to offer and will likely help all the time. Allow 20 minutes. Place the Post-it notes on the flipchart paper.
5. Ask for questions. Make sure that everyone is clear about the task. Reemphasize the importance of participation and sincerity. Remind everyone that they are free to read all the other notes for ideas and inspiration.
6. Get everyone back together in the circle and have participants volunteer to present the information written on the flipcharts.
7. Ask participants: What can we do to support each other in using that norm? What can we do when we aren't living up to that norm? Participants should write the answers to these questions on index cards, and then share their answers with the group at large.
8. Have the group discuss the various answers. Using a consensus process, participants should arrive at a list of actions that the group adopts in order to make sure that everyone supports each other.

Debriefing

• What did you learn about collaboration and about yourself from this activity?
• How can you use the product of this activity to enhance the collaborative nature of your team?
• What can you and your team do to improve its collaborative nature?

Variation

Conclude with a short imagining exercise:

Ask participants to close their eyes. Have them imagine that six months from now, they are in a group meeting. Imagine how living with the group norms will look. What have you been able to accomplish? How are you dealing with each other? What norms do you see in practice? Weave their norms into the story at this point by saying: How are you supporting honesty? What do you do if you think someone is being less than honest? and so on . . . Have them record their images on paper. Then let them break for coffee and encourage them to share their images with each other.

Activity 40

The Effective Team Member

A Consensus-Building Group-on-Group Activity

Purpose

1. To learn the characteristics of the effective team member
2. To learn the techniques of reaching a consensus decision
3. To learn how to observe team dynamics

Group Size

Up to twenty people

Time

2 hours

Physical Setting

A training room with two sets of chairs arranged in a circle. The result is a circle within a circle.

Materials

1. A copy of *Characteristics of an Effective Team Member* for each person
2. A copy of *Guidelines for Reaching a Consensus* for each person
3. A copy of *Team Member Characteristics Observation Guide* for each person

Process

1. Divide the group in half. A simple way to do this is to go around the group and have them count off "one, two, one, two . . ."
2. Have the "ones" form the inner circle and the "twos" form the outer circle. Each person from the outer circle is teamed up with one person from the inner circle. These teams of two meet briefly so the inner circle person can identify a few team member skills to improve upon, and which the outer circle person is to observe.
3. The outer circle people are given the *Team Member Characteristics Observation Guide* to help them observe the inner group. Under "other" they should add skills their partner wants to improve.
4. The inner group is given the *Characteristics of an Effective Team Member*. They are asked to work as a team and rank the characteristics in order of their importance to team effectiveness. Then they are asked to discuss and come up with a team consensus on the ranking of the characteristics. Allow 30 minutes. The outer circle members observe how their partners interact and take notes using the *Team Member Characteristics Observation Guide*.
5. The inner circle members meet with their outer circle partner to discuss and receive feedback on their participation with special emphasis on the areas they want to improve.
6. The outer circle team then gives general feedback to the inner group on the exercise. The facilitator leads a discussion on how to reach consensus.
7. *Guidelines for Reaching a Consensus* is distributed and reviewed.
8. Debrief the activity using the questions provided.

Debriefing

- What are some of the significant things that took place during this exercise?
- (For the outer group members) What did you learn about group dynamics from this experience? How will you apply these learnings in your work environment?
- (For the inner group members) What did you learn about being a team player from this experience? How will you apply these learnings in your work environment?
- What did you learn about reaching a consensus from this activity?
- What's the most important thing to keep in mind about reaching a team consensus?
- What norms should your team establish to help facilitate a consensus decision?

- If you were to participate in this exercise again, what would you do differently?

Variations

1. Have members of the inner circle portray specific team member characteristics. This should eliminate the observation feature of the activity where the outer circle person observes the behavior of one person in the inner circle. The observers would focus just on the team dynamics.
2. Extend the exercise by reversing the circles and having the outer circle move to the inner circle, and vice versa.
3. Have the groups switch and discuss the consensus activity they just observed. The new outer circle members become the observers of the new inner circle. The new outer circle members then provide feedback to the new inner circle.
4. Distribute *Guidelines for Reaching a Consensus* prior to the team consensus exercise. The team is instructed to use the guidelines during the exercise.
5. See Activity 46: Tough Jobs: A Consensus-Building Activity.

Team Member Characteristics Observation Guide

1. Encourages others to get involved: _____
   _____

2. Shares information and ideas: _____
   _____

3. Asks questions: _____
   _____

4. Is open to new ideas: _____
   _____

5. Uses good listening skills (e.g., paraphrasing): _____
   _____

6. Challenges assumptions: _____
   _____

7. Supports contributions of others: _____
   _____

8. Refocuses discussions (keeps group on track): _____
   _____

9. Summarizes the discussion: _____
   _____

10. Harmonizes conflict: _____
    _____

11. Other: _____
    _____

Characteristics of an Effective Team Member

Please rank the characteristics according to their importance to the success of the team. Each member of the team is to individually rank the items. Rank one as the most important and ten as the least important. After everyone has finished the individual ranking, rank the characteristics as a team.

Characteristics	Individual	Team
Encourages others to get involved	——————	——————
Shares information/ideas/opinions	——————	——————
Asks questions	——————	——————
Open to new ideas	——————	——————
Uses good listening skills	——————	——————
Challenges assumptions	——————	——————
Supports contributions of others	——————	——————
Refocuses discussions (keeps group on track)	——————	——————
Summarizes the discussion	——————	——————
Harmonizes conflicts	——————	——————

Guidelines for Reaching a Consensus

DOs

Use your active listening skills.
Research shows that teams with good listeners reach better decisions.

Involve everyone. The best way to get a good idea is to have lots of ideas.

Dig for facts. Seek out the reasons behind the opinions of your teammates.

DON'Ts

Horsetrade. "I'll give you number 3 but I want my number 4."

Vote. Voting creates "winners" and "losers."

Be afraid to rock the boat.
Constructive challenging often leads to better decisions.

Activity 41

The Product Development Team

A Simulation

Purpose

1. To experience a team planning process
2. To design and implement a team project
3. To learn to give and receive team feedback
4. To learn factors that help and hinder team decision-making

Group Size

A minimum of fifteen people. The activity is especially useful in a team-training workshop, but it can be used with an intact team.

Time

2 to 3 hours, depending on group size and the number of teams in the workshop

Physical Setting

Round or rectangular tables with chairs, spread out around the room. It is important that the teams be unable to hear each other during the session. If necessary, additional rooms can be used.

Materials

1. A copy of *Observer Guidelines* for each observer
2. A copy of *Team Reaction Form* for each participant
3. Easel, flipchart, and markers

Process

1. Form groups of six to seven people. Ask for two volunteers from each group to be observers.
2. Brief the observers privately using the *Observer Guidelines.*
3. While you are meeting with the observers, you may ask the teams to develop a set of norms for team effectiveness, which they will use during the exercise.
4. Ask each group to clear their table completely. Each group member is to place one item from a pocket or handbag on the table (e.g., coin, pen, key).
5. Explain that the task is to develop a competitive game that can be played by two people using only the objects on their table. They must also plan to teach the game to two people who will actually play the game. Allow 30 to 45 minutes.
6. When the time period is over, ask team members to complete the *Team Reaction Form.* Observers join the team members to give feedback and discuss the group's process during this period.
7. Have observers move to a table they did not observe. They are taught the game that was created by that group. They play the game and give the team feedback on the game.
8. The observers rejoin their original group. The teams discuss the feedback and they use the information to revise the game. The observers continue to record their observations. Allow 15 minutes.
9. Observers then go to another group they did not observe (a different one from the group they moved to in Step 7). They are now taught their game. They play the game and give feedback on the game to the group.
10. The observers return to their original group, where they share their experiences.
11. The facilitator debriefs the key learning points from this experience. The learning points are posted on the flipchart.
12. The facilitator concludes with a lecture on team planning, listening, roles, and decision-making.

Debriefing

- What did you learn about the importance and relationship between task and process in a team setting?
- In what ways was this project similar or different from the way you work back on the job?
- What did you learn from the observers' feedback?
- (For the observers) What did you learn from this experience?

Variations

1. Change Step 4 to give all teams the same items (e.g., paper clip, rubber band, watch, ring). The activity can be changed to a competitive exercise where the object is to create the best game.
2. A companion activity is Activity 45: Tricky Tales: A Cross-Team-Building Approach.

Worksheet

Observer Guidelines

1. Sit where you can see and hear most of the group.

2. Take notes. Include quotes where possible. Note the things that *help* the group and those things that *hinder* the group and the impact of what was said or done.

3. Look for data on:

    Task-Oriented Behavior (keeping focused on the job to be done): _____

    _____

    Strategic Behavior (seeing the big picture): _____

    _____

    Process Behavior (how the team is working together): _____

    _____

    Challenging Behavior (effectively disagreeing with others): _____

    _____

    Nonverbal Behavior (communicating without words): _____

    _____

    Dysfunctional Behavior (e.g., side conversations, monopolizing): _____

    _____

Worksheet

Team Reaction Form

1. How satisfied are you with the way your team planned the project?

   1   2   3   4   5

   Very   Very
   Dissatisfied   Satisfied

   Comments: _____

   _____

   _____

2. How satisfied are you with the way the team utilized its resources (both material and human)?

   1   2   3   4   5

   Very   Very
   Dissatisfied   Satisfied

   Comments: _____

   _____

   _____

3. Comment on the extent to which team members:

   a. Were focused on the task and shared their expertise: _____

   _____

   b. Saw the "big picture" and addressed strategic issues: _____

   _____

   c. Were concerned about team dynamics and positive process: _____

   _____

   d. Raised important questions about team goals and methods: _____

   _____

4. What things helped the team? _____

   _____

   _____

5. What things hindered team effectiveness? _____

_____

_____

6. How can we increase team effectiveness? _____

_____

_____

Activity 42

The Quality Case

An Ethical Dilemma

Purpose

1. To teach an ethical decision-making model for teams
2. To explore the factors involved in resolving an ethical dilemma

Group Size

Works best with team-building or team-training groups of four to twelve members

Time

1½ hours

Physical Setting

Round or rectangular tables with chairs

Materials

1. A copy of *Factors in Team Ethics* for each person
2. A copy of *The Quality Case* for each person
3. Flipchart, markers, and masking tape or push pins

Process

1. Explain the purpose of the exercise. Brainstorm either "ethical issues we face as a team" or "ethical issues faced by teams." Discuss the list but do not attempt to reduce it.
2. Distribute *Factors in Team Ethics*. Review and explain each factor. Ask the participants for examples that illustrate each factor (e.g., "What laws and regulations affect our work?")
3. Distribute *The Quality Case*. Ask the team to analyze the case and decide what they would do. The team should use the *Factors in Team Ethics* handout as a guide in analyzing the case.
4. The team presents its analysis and decision. Group discussion follows, with the facilitator probing for reasons and other alternatives.
5. Return to the list of issues generated in Step 3. The facilitator asks the team to suggest norms that address the ethical issues that emerge from this exercise. The norms are posted on the flipchart.
6. Debrief the activity using the questions provided.

Debriefing

*   What insights did you gain relevant to ethics and decision-making as a result of participating in this activity?
*   What possible ethical dilemmas do you believe your team faces as it strives to achieve its mission?
*   Do you think there is a difference between ethics and judgment?

Variations

1. Revise the case, or create a new case that more closely relates to the work of the team.
2. The team analyzes the case prior to the presentation of the *Factors in Team Ethics* handout. Review the handout after the team presents its solution. Discuss the case again in light of the factors.

Worksheet

The Quality Case

Your team is responsible for the development of a new system. The team has contracted with a user group for a specific set of requirements and delivery date.

At a team meeting just prior to the delivery date, several team members argue that the system is not up to their usual standards of quality. They do not want to deploy the system because it still has some problems. Other team members want to deliver the system on the due date in order to meet the commitment. They say that while it still has some problems, it does meet the user's requirements. The others agree that the system does, in fact, meet the requirements, but they say that the team should not allow work of questionable quality to "go public."

1. What is the dilemma?

   _____

   _____

   _____

   _____

2. Who are the stakeholders?

   _____

   _____

   _____

   _____

3. What factors should the team consider in making its decision?

   _____

   _____

   _____

   _____

4. What should the team do?

_____

_____

_____

_____

Factors in Team Ethics

1. Laws and regulations

2. Professional standards and ethical codes of conduct

3. Corporate policies and procedures

4. Corporate culture and organizational norms

5. Personal and team values

Activity 43

The Way We Are, and Want to Be

A Visioning Activity for an Intact Team

Purpose

1. To develop a shared vision for an intact team
2. To prepare a common statement that describes the current state of the team

Group Size

Designed for an intact team of fewer than ten members. However, it can be adapted for a session in which a number of intact teams come together but work independently on the activity.

Time

1½ hours

Physical Setting

Comfortable chairs in a circle or set around a small conference table

Materials

1. Flipchart stand with full pad of paper
2. A supply of markers in a variety of colors
3. Masking tape or push pins
4. A copy of the *A Vision is . . .* handout for each person
5. *Optional:* A variety of industry magazines that contain advertisements with lots of pictures, a pair of scissors, and a bottle of glue or paste for each team member

Process

1. Introduce the exercise by explaining the importance of having a direction for the team—something beyond short-term goals and action plans. Explain the concept of vision. Use the *A Vision Is . . .* handout to facilitate the discussion.
2. Give team members a sheet of flipchart paper and some markers and ask them to create their vision of the team one year from now. As an alternative, you can provide them with industry magazines to illustrate their vision. Be careful to explain that they can use pictures, graphics, symbols, or words to create their vision. Explain further that artistic ability is not a consideration in this activity. Allow 20-30 minutes.
3. Ask each person to post their vision on the wall around the room. Then ask team members to view the "exhibit" looking for:

   - Similarities
   - Differences
   - Surprises

4. Facilitate a discussion that focuses on creating a shared vision that emerges from the various individual member visions. Record the responses on the flipchart. The product should be a consensus statement of the team's vision. Members of the team should be comfortable saying that the vision is the future they want to work toward.
5. Distribute another sheet of paper and ask team members to individually prepare their view of the team at this moment in time. Allow 15 minutes. Once again, ask the team members to post their products on the wall (adjacent to their visions).
6. Have team members walk around and view the "exhibit." Facilitate a discussion on similarities, differences, and surprises. Conclude the discussion with the development of a common view of the current state of the team.

7. Take a break at this point to allow the results to incubate.
8. Conclude the activity with the development of an action plan to get from the current state to the vision. Post the elements on the flipchart. If the team seems ready, form subgroups to tackle various elements.

Debriefing

- How comfortable were you with the visioning exercise?
- What did you learn from this exercise?
- In what ways can you personally use the results of the exercise?
- How would you describe the way the team worked on this exercise?
- Beyond the obvious (i.e., we created a plan), in what ways did the team benefit from this exercise?
- If you were to do this exercise again in the future, how would you do it?

Variations

1. Ask team members to do some prework to prepare for the activity by asking each person to think about things he or she would like to see the team do or be in the future.
2. Incorporate a team-assessment survey in the activity, either as a supplement to or substitute for the picture of the current state of the team in Step 5. One such survey is the *Team Development Survey* by Glenn Parker.*
3. Direct team members to use the top half of the flipchart paper for the vision (Step 2) and the bottom for the current state (Step 5).

*Available from Consulting Psychologists Press at 800-624-1765.

Worksheet

A Vision Is . . .

. . . a picture or statement of your *desired* future, rather than your *predicted* future.

. . . what you *hope* the future will be, rather than what you *think* it will be.

. . . your hopes . . . your dreams . . . your aspirations . . . your "druthers."

. . . where you want to be.

. . . something to rally around—a glue that pulls the team together.

. . . a challenge to achieve a higher purpose than just getting product out the door or responding to customer requests.

. . . as vague as a dream, or as precise as a goal.

Activity 44

TMS

A Process for Role Clarification

Purpose

1. To clarify the roles played in a team
2. To clarify expectations of other members and themselves
3. To understand the process of role adjustment

Group Size

No more than twelve members of an intact team

Time

2 hours

Physical Setting

A private room, with wall space for posting flipcharts

Materials

1. Easel, flipchart, markers, and masking tape or push pins
2. A copy of the *TMS Questionnaire* for each person

3. A copy of the *TMS Questionnaire: Interpretation Guide* for each person
4. Paper and pen for team members

Process

1. The facilitator presents a lecture on the three elements of the TMS Model: Task-Oriented Roles, Maintenance-Oriented Roles, and Self-Oriented Roles.
2. The facilitator asks the members to complete the *TMS Questionnaire* for themselves only.
3. The facilitator asks the group for a volunteer.
4. The facilitator asks the members to complete a *TMS Questionnaire* for the volunteer.
5. The volunteer then guesses what the other members of the team have said.
6. The volunteer then questions the other team members and records their actual responses.
7. The facilitator leads a discussion of the responses.
8. The volunteer and team members engage in a discussion of the results guided by the facilitator.
9. The facilitator conducts a renegotiation, resulting in a new contract between the volunteer and fellow team members.
10. Steps 3 to 9 are repeated until all team members have a chance to participate.
11. The team can create a composite team score on the questionnaire.
12. The *TMS Questionnaire: Interpretation Guide* can be used by the facilitator to help the team understand the impact of task-, maintenance-, and self-oriented roles on the effectiveness of a team.

Debriefing

- What are some of the significant things that took place during this activity?
- How will you use the information from discussions to improve your team's effectiveness?
- What's the most important personal insight you gained from this activity?

Variations

1. Each team member can complete the *TMS Questionnaire* for themselves and the other team members prior to the meeting.
2. Another role clarification exercise is Activity 4: Choice Role: A Role-Clarification Activity.

TMS Questionnaire

Task-Oriented Roles • Maintenance-Oriented Roles • Self-Oriented Roles

Task-oriented roles contribute to the ability of the group to accomplish its objective.

	Low				High
1. Initiating interaction	1	2	3	4	5
2. Giving/Seeking information	1	2	3	4	5
3. Giving/Seeking opinions	1	2	3	4	5
4. Clarifying	1	2	3	4	5
5. Summarizing	1	2	3	4	5

Maintenance-oriented roles contribute to the ability of the team to create and maintain effective interpersonal relations.

	Low				High
1. Harmonizing	1	2	3	4	5
2. Compromising	1	2	3	4	5
3. Supporting	1	2	3	4	5
4. Gatekeeping	1	2	3	4	5
5. Encouraging	1	2	3	4	5

Self-oriented roles do not contribute to the effectiveness of the team.

	Low				High
1. Blocking	1	2	3	4	5
2. Withdrawing	1	2	3	4	5
3. Dominating	1	2	3	4	5
4. Being aggressive	1	2	3	4	5
5. Criticizing	1	2	3	4	5

TMS Questionnaire: Interpretation Guide

The *TMS Questionnaire Interpretation Guide* provides insight for understanding your team's data.

Task-Oriented Roles

Scores from 5 to 10 indicate that task roles are having a negative impact on the team's ability to accomplish its objectives. There might be a lack of communication, an unwillingness to share information, or a weakness in creating action or follow-through plans. The team should reevaluate its norms and process, and develop a new working contract.

Scores from 11 to 15 indicate that the task roles are moving from a positive or neutral position to a negative position, and should tell the team that it's time to reexamine its structure.
Scores from 16 to 20 indicate that the team is fairly healthy, and that periodic check-ups would help keep the team on track.

Scores above 20 indicate a team that is well on its way to achieving its goals.

Maintenance-Oriented Roles

Scores from 5 to 10 indicate that maintenance roles are having a negative impact on the team's ability to accomplish its objectives. There may be a lack of concern for team members, some discounting of one another, poor communication patterns, or little support for fellow team members. The team should reevaluate its norms and communication process, and establish stronger working norms.

Scores from 11 to 15 indicate that the task roles are moving from a positive or neutral position to a negative position, and should tell the team that it's time to reexamine its interpersonal relationships.

Scores from of 16 to 20 indicate that the team is fairly healthy, and that periodic check-ups would help keep the team on track.

Scores above 20 indicate a team that is well on its way to achieving its goals.

Self-Oriented Roles

Scores from 5 to 10 indicate that self-oriented roles are having a negative impact on the team's ability to accomplish its objectives. There might be a set of personal agendas at work, a lack of concern for team members, some discounting of one another, poor communication patterns, or little support for fellow team members. The team should reevaluate its norms and communication process, and establish stronger working norms.

Scores from 11 to 15 indicate that the task roles are moving from a positive or neutral position to a negative position and should tell the team members that it's time to reexamine their personal commitment to the team, its interpersonal relationships, and the contribution each member is making to the team's success.

Scores from 16 to 20 indicate that the team and its members are fairly healthy, and that periodic check-ups would help keep the team on track.

Scores above 20 indicate a team that is well on its way to achieving its goals.

Activity 45

Tricky Tales

A Cross-Team-Building Approach

Purpose

1. To learn the difference between competitive and collaborative team behavior
2. To learn the techniques of cross-team teamwork

Group Size

A minimum of sixteen people. If you have fewer people, use only three tales.

Time

2 hours

Physical Setting

A large room, with four round or rectangular tables and chairs spread out around the room so that the teams can have some privacy

Materials

1. Four envelopes containing 3 × 5 index cards prepared according to the *Directions for Preparing the Tricky Tales*

279

2. A copy of *Observer Guidelines* for each observer
3. A copy of *Teamwork Guidelines* for each person
4. A copy of *Tricky Tales* for each participant
5. A copy of the *Answer Key* for each person
6. Lecture notes for the facilitator. (You might wish to make this into an overhead, in which case you would need the overhead transparency, an overhead projector, and markers.)

Process

1. Form four teams of at least four people each. Designate the teams 1, 2, 3, and 4. Ask one person from each team to volunteer to be an observer. Brief the observer using the *Observer Guidelines.*
2. Review the *Teamwork Guidelines* with the whole group. The facilitator explains that the four groups must work together to create four tales using the clues in the envelopes. Then each group must find the answer to their tale. Distribute the premade envelopes to the four teams.
3. The facilitator makes it clear that the activity is not over until all four teams have all the clues needed for their tale and the correct answer to their tale.
4. The facilitator will confirm the answer (hand out copies of *Tricky Tales* and the *Answer Key*) only after the groups have correctly assembled all the clues and have correctly solved the tale.
5. When everyone is finished, the observers provide feedback to their team and lead a discussion on the things that helped and hindered the process.
6. The facilitator debriefs the exercise, focusing on how teams can work effectively with other teams.
7. The session concludes with a lecture on cross-team teamwork.
8. Debrief the activity using the questions below.

Debriefing

- What did you see happen during the activity?
- How do you feel about what happened?
- When you first started, what did you think was the purpose of the exercise?
- What happened to cause you to realize that the way to "win" was to collaborate with the other teams?
- What did you learn about teamwork from this experience?
- What are some parallel situations in your organization?
- What are the real-time barriers to cross-team collaboration in your organization?

- What are some of the things that you have done to facilitate cross-team collaboration?

Variations

1. The activity can be made competitive by changing the directions to indicate that the first team to obtain all their clues and answer the tale is the winner.
2. The facilitator can pull the observers into a circle in the center of the room for a discussion of their observations and learning on cross-team teamwork.
3. The tales can be changed to problems that are related to the work of the teams.
4. See Activity 41: The Product Development Team: A Simulation for a similar activity.

Directions for Preparing the Tricky Tales

Print each clue below on a 3 × 5 card. Do not include the numbers on the 3 × 5 cards. The numbers are included to make sure the cards are distributed across the four groups. Place all cards labeled "1" in an envelope marked "1" and so on for the remaining three sets of cards. You should have four envelopes marked 1, 2, 3, and 4.

Tale 1

4   Mr. Smith and his son are driving in a car.
3   The car crashed.
1   The father was instantly killed.
2   The son was critically injured and rushed to the hospital.
1   The surgeon took a look at him and said, "I can't operate on him. He is my son, Arthur."
2   How do you explain this?

Tale 2

1   A grocer has some apples for sale.
3   One customer buys one-half of all the apples plus half of an apple.
3   A second customer takes one-half of the remaining apples plus half of an apple.
2   The third customer purchases one half of the quantity left plus half of an apple.
1   The grocer is now completely sold out.
3   None of the customers bought fractions of apples.
2   All purchases were whole numbers of apples.
1   How many apples did the grocer originally have?

Tale 3

1   Two people own a horse.
2   The both insist that their horse is the slowest.
3   They were going to have a race to settle the argument, but neither person would trust that the other would ride to the fullest without the slightest holding back of the horse.
1   How can the slowest horse be definitely established?

Tale 4

2   There are twelve white socks and forty-nine red socks, all mixed up in a drawer.
3   These are individual socks, not pairs.
1   All socks are the same size and made of the same material, so no distinction can be made by any of your senses.
4   What is the minimum number of socks you must pull out of the drawer, with your eyes closed, to make sure one matching pair was among those chosen?

Observer Guidelines

1. Sit where you can see and hear most of the team.
2. Take notes. Include quotes where possible. Note the things that *help* and the things that *hinder* the team, and the impact of what was said or done.
3. Look for data on:

Competitive Behavior (working against the other teams): _____

_____

Collaborative Behavior (working with the other teams): _____

_____

Task-Oriented Behavior (keeping focused on the job to be done): _____

_____

Strategic Behavior (seeing the big picture): _____

_____

Process Behavior (how the team is working together): _____

_____

Challenging Behavior (effectively disagreeing with others): _____

_____

Nonverbal Behavior (communicating without words): _____

_____

Dysfunctional Behavior (e.g., side conversations, monopolizing): _____

_____

Comments: _____

_____

Worksheet

Teamwork Guidelines

Task

The team is to solve the tale. To accomplish this task, each team must do two things: (1) obtain all clues and (2) determine the correct solution. The solution must not be submitted until all of the clues of the tale are in the team's possession. The facilitator will tell you if you have all the clues and whether or not your answer is correct.

Procedure

To obtain all the clues, you negotiate with the other three teams for the clues. The rules for negotiation are:

1. Only one member of a team may leave the team at any one time.
2. Only one member may negotiate with any team at any one time.
3. Each member of the team must have at least one opportunity to negotiate with another team.
4. No more than two clues may be exchanged during any transaction with another team.

orksheet

Tricky Tales

The Car Crash

A Mr. Smith and his son were driving in a car. The car crashed. The father was killed instantly. The son was critically injured and rushed to the hospital. The surgeon took a look at him and said, "I can't operate on him. He is my son, Arthur." How do you explain this?

How 'Bout Them Apples

A grocer has some apples for sale. One customer buys one-half of all the apples plus half of an apple. A second customer takes one-half of the remaining apples plus a half an apple. The third customer purchases one half of the quantity left plus a half an apple. The grocer is now completely sold out. None of the customers bought fractions of apples. All purchases were whole numbers of apples. How many apples did the grocer originally have?

The Loser Is a Winner

Each of two people owns a horse. They both insist that their horse is the slowest. They were going to have a race to settle the argument, but neither person would trust that the other would ride to the fullest without the slightest holding back of the horse. How can the slowest horse be definitely established?

Sox Fox

There are twelve white socks and forty-nine red socks all mixed up in a drawer. These are individual socks, not pairs. What is the minimum number of socks you must pull out of the drawer, with your eyes closed, to make sure one matching pair was among those chosen? All socks are the same size and made of the same material, so no distinctions can be made by your senses.

Answer Key

1. **The Car Crash**
   The surgeon was Arthur's mother.

2. **How 'Bout Them Apples**
   The grocer originally had seven apples.

3. **The Loser Is the Winner**
   Each person rides the other person's horse in a race.

4. **Sox Fox**
   If you take three socks from the drawer, two of the three must match, since only two colors exist.

Lecture Notes: **CROSS-TEAM COLLABORATION**

Barriers to Cross-Team Collaboration

- **Stereotyping.** We make assumptions about people on other teams.
- **Competition.** Teams often believe they are in competition with each other.
- **Lack of Information.** We often lack information about the other team's goals, culture, and operating procedures.
- **Lack of Skill.** Teams do not know how to collaborate with each other.

How to Facilitate Effective Cross-Team Collaboration

- **Develop a Common Objective.** Create an "umbrella" that all groups can get under.
- **Provide Information.** Information about the teams can break down barriers.
- **Establish Mechanisms.** Share team minutes, attend each other's meetings, give presentations to each other, and develop joint projects.
- **Select Boundary Managers.** Carefully select the people who represent your team with other teams.
- **Develop Trust.** Honor commitments, provide honest data, and don't overpromise.

Activity 46

Tough Jobs

A Consensus-Building Activity

Purpose

1. To assess the degree to which members of a team can agree on a set of data
2. To teach the process of consensus decision-making

Group Size

Effective either as a team-building activity with an intact team of five to seven people or in a team-training workshop with several teams of five to seven people

---

Time

2 hours

Physical Setting

A room large enough for several break-out sessions of five to seven people each

---

Materials

1. A copy of the *Tough Jobs Ranking Sheet* for each person
2. A flipchart and markers

3. A copy of the *Consensus Decision-Making Process Review* for each person
4. A copy of the *Tough Jobs Answer Sheet* for each person
5. A copy of *Using the Consensus Method* for the facilitator

Process

1. The facilitator forms groups.
2. Each team member is given a *Tough Jobs Ranking Sheet* and is asked to privately rank the jobs according to the degree of danger in the job. The most dangerous job is ranked "1" and so on with the rank of "10" for the least dangerous job.
3. Once the individual rankings have been completed, the team is asked to develop a team ranking of the jobs. Allow 30 minutes.
4. Distribute *Consensus Decision-Making Process Review*. Ask each person to complete the form, but not to discuss it.
5. Present the *Tough Jobs Answer Sheet*. The answers should be listed in column 3 on the ranking sheet. Ask the team to complete columns 4 and 5 including the totals. Ask a person on each team to compute the average individual score by adding the individual scores (column 4) and dividing by the number of team members.
6. Post a flipchart with the scores from each team as follows:

	Team A	*Team B*	*Team C*
Average Individual Score			
Team Score (column 5)			
Difference			

7. The facilitator should lead a discussion on the reasons for the difference between the average individual score and the team score. See instructions under *Debriefing*.
8. Debrief the activity using the *Consensus Decision-Making Process Review* form.
9. The facilitator concludes the session with a debriefing on the learnings from the activity and a lecture on consensus decision-making. Use the lecture notes *Using the Consensus Method*.

Debriefing

- Distribute the *Consensus Decision-Making Process Review* form. Ask each person to complete the form. When the time comes, facilitate a discussion based on the questions. Post the responses to questions three and four on the flipchart. Probe for further understanding and implications of the responses. If there are subgroups, ask one person to serve as the facilitator in each group.

- You may also ask:
  —What did you learn about consensus today?
  —How will you apply the learning points?
  —When is consensus most appropriate as a team decision-making method?
  —When is consensus not useful?

Variations

1. Another consensus activity is Activity 40: The Effective Team Member: A Consensus-Building Group-on-Group Activity.
2. You can create your own consensus activity by going to *The Book of Lists*.

Tough Jobs Ranking Sheet

	1 *Your individual ranking*	2 *The team's ranking*	3 *Expert's ranking*	4 *Difference between steps 1 & 3*	5 *Difference between steps 2 & 3*
1. Agricultural worker					
2. Police officer					
3. Deep-sea diver					
4. Construction worker					
5. Rancher					
6. Welder					
7. Chemical worker					
8. Miner					
9. Trawler person					
10. Firefighter					
			Total	Your score	Team score

Consensus Decision-Making Process Review

Reflect on this activity for a few minutes.

1. What helped the team reach a consensus?

_____

_____

_____

_____

2. What hindered the team?

_____

_____

_____

_____

3. What should the team do to increase its effectiveness in achieving a consensus?

_____

_____

_____

4. What can you do to increase the effectiveness of the team in achieving a consensus?

_____

_____

_____

Worksheet

Tough Jobs Answer Sheet

1. Deep-sea diver

2. Trawler person

3. Miner

4. Construction worker

5. Agricultural worker

6. Welder

7. Chemical worker

8. Police officer

9. Firefighter

10. Rancher

From: *The People's Almanac,* 1988.

Lecture Notes: **USING THE CONSENSUS METHOD**

DOs	*DON'Ts*
Use your active listening skills. Research shows that teams with good listeners reach better decisions.	**Horse trade.** "I'll give you number 3, but I want my number 4."
Involve everyone. The best way to get a good idea is to have lots of ideas.	**Vote.** Voting creates "winners" and "losers."
Dig for facts. Seek out the reasons behind the opinions of your teammates.	**Be afraid to rock the boat!** Constructive challenging often leads to better decisions.

Activity 47

Virtual Brainstorming

Problem-Solving for a Geographically Dispersed Team

Purpose

1. To generate ideas among team members who come from different locations
2. To use e-mail to develop a prioritized list of ideas

Group Size

Unlimited; however, the activity works best with an intact team of less than fifteen and all must be able to communicate via e-mail

Time

We recommend that the total process be completed in approximately 7 days

Physical Setting

No meeting room or equipment is required

Materials

No printed materials are needed. The information required for the activity is found in *Virtual Brainstorming Guidelines* and here in the procedures.

Process

1. The team leader or facilitator selects a clear topic area for brainstorming such as:

   • Ways to improve the operation of the customer service center.
   • Communication problems between the second and third shifts.
   • Ideas for improving our relationship with systems engineering.

2. The leader sends the topic to all team members in an e-mail message, and asks each person to do a private "brainstorm" of responses. In the e-mail message, team members are asked to submit their list of ideas to the leader. Be sure to include a deadline (e.g., two days). If team members are unfamiliar with brainstorming, send our *Virtual Brainstorming Guidelines*.

3. The leader compiles a list of all the responses and sends it back out to the members. No names are included with the list. Members are asked to vote for the three best ideas and send their responses back to the leader. Include a deadline (e.g., two days) for submission of their votes.

4. The leader tallies the votes and sends the rank-order list out to the members. The list includes the number of votes received for each item on the list.

Debriefing

• The leader might want to send these questions out to team members to get their input on the process. In this case, the responses should be sent simultaneously to all members, rather than just to the leader.
   —How did you feel about the process?
   —How different was this brainstorming activity from one where everyone is in the same room?
   —What were the advantages of this activity?
   —What were the disadvantages?
   —How should we do it differently in the future?
   —How would the results have changed if you had known who authored each item on the list before you voted?

Variations

1. Post the names of the team members who authored the three top-rated ideas. Give each of these people a small prize.

2. When team members vote for the best ideas, ask them to also "predict" which items they believe will receive the highest number of votes. Give a small prize to the people who correctly guess the winners.

3. One approach used by some teams includes asking subgroups to take one of the top-rated items and develop an action plan for implementation.

We acknowledge our colleague, Sivasailam "Thiagi" Thiagarajan, for his development of this concept.

Virtual Brainstorming Guidelines

1. You may submit as many ideas as you like—there is no limit to the number of ideas.

2. You may submit your ideas in several different e-mails, as long as they meet the deadline.

3. Do not evaluate or prejudge your ideas—the wilder and wackier the better.

4. Build on your own ideas—you can even submit ideas that are extensions or modifications of other ideas already submitted.

5. Other team members will not know who authored the ideas—the leader will send out the list with no names attached.

6. Our goal is to get lots of ideas—so let yourself go!

Facilitator: Guideline 5 should be omitted if you use variation 1 of the activity.

Activity 48

Virtual Consensus

Participative Decision-Making without a Meeting

Purpose

1. To come to an agreement or make a team decision without a face-to-face or teleconference meeting
2. To help a team learn to use the consensus method
3. To use e-mail as a learning and decision-making tool
4. To add some fun to a consensus decision-making process

Group Size

The number of participants is unlimited, but all must be able to communicate with each other via e-mail

Time

We suggest that you ask team members to respond within 2 days, but you may increase or decrease the time limit based on existing team norms.

Physical Setting

Since members are not meeting at the same time and the same place, this activity simply requires that all members be able to communicate with each other via e-mail.

Materials

No printed materials are needed. The information required for the activity is found in step 3 of the Process.

Process

1. This activity is used when a team must make a decision that does not require a great deal of explanation or discussion and in situations where you do not expect a great deal of controversy. Typical decisions might include approval of a final report, agreement on the agenda for a project review or approval of proposed reporting process.
2. Send an e-mail to each participant describing the decision to be made or providing a copy of the document as an attachment.
3. In the same e-mail message, provide the following decision options:

   - I can say an unqualified "yes" to the proposed decision.
   - I find the decision acceptable.
   - I can live with the decision, but I'm not especially enthusiastic about it.
   - I do not fully agree with the decision, but I do not choose to block it.
   - I do not agree with the decision, and I feel we should explore other options.

4. Ask each team member to selection one option and hit the reply button with his or her response.
5. Compile the responses, and if most of the members select one of the first four responses, you have a virtual consensus. If many people select the fifth option, you have misjudged the situation. You need a real-time meeting to resolve the issue.
6. Provide the team with a summary of the responses indicating how many votes each option received.

Variation

Add some fun by making a game out of the exercise. Ask each person to also provide you with his or her guess as to which option will receive the most votes and how many votes the winning option will receive. Give prizes to the people who selected the winning option and a larger prize to the person who correctly the guessed the number of votes the winning option would receive.

Activity 49

Wisdom

An Intergroup Team Game

Purpose

To demonstrate the value of cross-group collaboration

Group Size

This activity works best with three groups of four to six members each, plus one process observer for each group. If you have more people, you can do some or all of the following:

- You can create a fourth group. This will require preparing the handout so that the clues are spread out over four groups.
- You can use two process observers for each group.
- You can increase the group size to seven or eight people.

Time

45 minutes

Physical Setting

Chairs arranged around a small table for each group. The tables and chairs should be set around the room so that each group can work in private.

Materials

1. A copy of the *Wisdom Game Instructions* handout for each group
2. A copy of the appropriate *Wisdom Team Task* handout for each group (Group 1 receives the handout designated for Group 1, etc.)
3. A copy of the *Wisdom Process Observer Guidelines* for each group observer
4. Flipchart and markers

Process

1. Open the session by explaining that the purpose of the activity is to give each group an opportunity to practice working as a team on a task. It will be an opportunity to apply some of their individual team-player skills and overall team-building tools. Do not reveal the goal of fostering cross-team collaboration. You want them to discover this goal on their own.
2. Distribute the *Wisdom Game Instructions* to each person. Review the instructions and the sample sentence. Give each group a few minutes to figure out the answer to the sample sentence. ("There is no I in *team*.")
3. Distribute the appropriate *Wisdom Team Task* to each group. Indicate that they will have 10 minutes to complete the task. Ask for one volunteer from each group to serve as a process observer. Distribute the *Wisdom Process Observers Guidelines.*
4. At the end of 10 minutes, begin the debriefing of the activity using some of the questions presented in the next section.

Debriefing

- How do you feel about the experience?
- How satisfied are you with the way your group went about completing the task?
- When and how did you decide to collaborate with the other groups?
- (If you did not collaborate with the other groups.) Why didn't you work with the other groups to complete the task?
- What does this activity tell you about cross-group collaboration?
- How is the way you approached this task different from or similar to the way you work back home on the job?
- Why do we often assume that when we play a game, only one team can win?
- Why did you assume that you were competing against the other groups?

- If I had said that more than one team could win, would that have changed the way you went about completing the task?
- How can we break down the barriers that keep us from collaborating with other groups?
- What learning points about teamwork will you take away from this activity?
- How will you apply those learning points back on the job?

Variations

1. Add prizes for completing the task on time. Tell the groups in advance that there will be prizes for completing the task in 5 minutes or 10 minutes.
2. Change the Wisdom sentence to something relevant to your organization (e.g., company advertising slogan).

Wisdom Game Instructions

Task

Your task is to fill in the blanks and complete the sentence correctly.

All groups have the same sentence, but their clues are different.

You may organize yourself in any way and use any means to complete the task.

Time Limit

You have 5 minutes to complete the task.

Scoring

If you complete the task in 3 minutes, you will receive 50 points.

If you complete the task in 5 minutes, you will receive 30 points.

Sample

```
        __ H __ __ __
              __ S
            N O
               .
              __
            I __
        __ E __ __ M
```

Wisdom Team Task

GROUP 1

I __

__ O __

__ __ N ' __

__ N O __

__ __ E __ __

__ __ __

A R E

G __ __ __ __

__ __ __

__ __ A D

__ I __ __

__ A __ __

Y O U

__ __ __ __ __

Worksheet

Wisdom Team Task

GROUP 2

```
        __ F
     __ __ U
  __ __ __ T
K __ __ __
W H __ __ __
  Y __ __

   __ __ __
  __ __ I N G

   __ __ __
R __ __ __
W __ __ L
__ __ K __

   __ __ __
T H E __ __
```

Wisdom Team Task

GROUP 3

```
        — —
      Y — —
    D O — —
    — — — W
    — — — R E
      — O U
      — — —
    — O — — —
      A N Y
    — O — —
    — — L —
    T — — E
      — — —
    — — — R E
```

Wisdom Process Observer Guidelines

Instructions: Please sit where you can see and hear the group clearly. You should be outside of the group. Do not speak to any group members once the activity begins. Take notes, using the topics and questions below as a guide. Feel free to note anything else you believe is significant. You are looking for behaviors that help or hinder the team as it goes about completing the task.

1. **Task focus**. What did group members do to help get the task completed? What got in the way of the group's ability to complete the task?

   _____

   _____

   _____

   _____

2. **Relationship focus.** How would you describe interpersonal relationships among group members? Did you see any indications of encouraging participation, making supportive comments, managing disagreements, building consensus, or listening actively?

   _____

   _____

   _____

3. **Competition**. To what extent did the group seem to be competing with the other groups? Were they trying to win?

   _____

   _____

   _____

4. **Collaboration.** Did anyone in the group suggest collaborating with the other groups? Did anyone recognize that the other groups had different clues?

_____

_____

_____

5. **Other observations.** Did you observe any other behaviors that either helped or hindered the group's efforts to complete the task?

_____

_____

_____

Activity 50

Yea, Team!

A Large-Group Icebreaker

Purpose

1. To open a team-training workshop with an energizing activity
2. To help participants who are unfamiliar with each other to get acquainted

---

Group Size

A minimum of twenty people is required. There is no maximum number. The activity can be done with a smaller group if the number of boxes on the grid is reduced.

Time

45 minutes

Physical Setting

A large room or section of a room that allows the participants to move around easily

---

Materials

1. A copy of the *Team Grid* for each person
2. Pencils or pens for each person

Process

1. Prior to the session, find out information about the people in the group—hobbies, interests, past experiences, accomplishments, or unusual facts. You can use items from the sample "Yea, Team!" grid.
2. Explain the purpose of the activity. Distribute a copy of the *Team Grid*.
3. Explain the guidelines: The leader calls out items about people in the group and the participants randomly write the items in boxes on the *Grid*. A few boxes can be designated as wild cards. Each box should have an item in it.
4. Participants walk around the room and find people who are or can do the items in the boxes. When they find someone who fits the description, they ask the person to sign or initial that box. Participants try to get as many boxes signed as possible in the time available. However, people are encouraged to ask follow-up questions to find out more about the item from the person. A person may only sign one box on your grid, even though several items may apply to them. You may not sign your own grid. Allow 20 minutes.
5. The team reassembles. The leader explains that the goal is to spell *Team*. The first person to spell Team is the winner. The leader says "Put 'T' in box number ___. You may put a T in that box only if you have a signature in the box." The leader continues calling out " 'E' in box number ___, 'A' in box number ___, 'M' in box number ___" until someone in the group can spell Team on their *Team Grid*. The person yells out "Yea, Team!" and is declared the winner. You may continue to play until there are three winners. We suggest prizes for the winners such as T-shirts, sweatshirts, or hats.
6. Debrief the activity using the questions below.

Debriefing

- What new things did you learn about people in this group?
- What things surprised you?
- How does this information help you?
- How does this activity help your team?

A different way to debrief this activity is to ask people about the items in the grid. For example:

- Who plays a musical instrument? What do you play?
- Who has met someone famous? Who was it?

A software program called ZINGO allows you to easily create custom grids. ZINGO is available from Workshops by Thiagi, 4423 East Trailridge Road, Bloomington, IN 47408 (812-332-1478).

- Who does volunteer work? What type of work?
- Who is a risk-taker? What's the riskiest thing you've ever done?

Variations

1. Tailor the items for the boxes to the people in the group.
2. If the group is small, after the activity, ask people to introduce themselves by incorporating the items from the grid.
3. Create teams using items from the grid. For example, all people who like to ski move to a corner of the room to discuss their interests. Then move on to related team issues.

Worksheet

Team Grid

1	2	3	4	5
6	7	8	9	10
11	12	13	14	15
16	17	18	19	20
21	22	23	24	25

Worksheet — *Yea, Team!*

Likes to ski	Has three children	Plays a musical instrument	Always prepared for an "emergency"	First or only child
Has performed on stage	Been with the company 10+ years	Native of the "Windy City"	Survived an earthquake	Has met someone famous
Absent-minded professor	A chocoholic	A good kisser	Can name the seven dwarfs	Soccer mom
Rides a Harley	Collects antiques	Car show fanatic	Likes to tie flies	Does volunteer work
Went to school in Europe	Has a rich fantasy life	A runner or jogger	Owns a Corvette	New kid on the block

Team Workout Resources

Books

D. L. Duarte and N. T. Snyder, *Mastering Virtual Teams;* Jossey-Bass, 1999.

J. R. Hackman (ed.), *Groups That Work (and Those That Don't);* Jossey-Bass, 1990.

J. Katzenbach and D. Smith, *The Wisdom of Teams;* Harvard Business School Press, 1993.

G. M. Parker, *Team Players and Teamwork;* Jossey-Bass, 1990, 1995.

G. M. Parker, *Cross-Functional Teams: Working with Allies, Enemies, and Other Strangers;* Jossey-Bass, 1994.

G. Parker, J. McAdams and D. Zielinski, *Rewarding Teams: Lessons from the Trenches;* Jossey-Bass, 2000.

Facilitator Handbooks

G. M. Parker and R. P. Kropp, Jr., *50 Activities for Self-Directed Teams;* HRD Press, 1994.

G. M. Parker, *25 Instruments for Team Building;* HRD Press, 1998.

M. Silberman, *101 Ways to Make Meetings Active;* Pfeiffer, 1999.

P. R. Scholtes and Others, *The Team Handbook;* Joiner Associates, 1988.

S. Thiagarajan and G. Parker, *Teamwork and Teamplay: Games and Activities for Building and Training Teams;* Pfeiffer, 1999.

L. Ukens, *All Together Now!* Pfeiffer, 1999.

Web Sites

Glenn Parker. In addition to describing Glenn's products and services, the site has a freebies section that includes downloadable exercises and articles on teams and a user's group for the *Parker Team Player Survey.* (www.glennparker.com)

Dick Kropp. This site describes Dick's products and services, which include training and development, human resources planning, and e-commerce. You can purchase team-building products online. (www.kroppgroup.com)

Workshops by Thiagi. An internationally recognized provider of consulting, training, and publications with an emphasis on games and simulations for team building. Lots of free exercises are available. (www.thiagi.com)

University of North Texas, Center for the Study of Work Teams. The Center is a leader in providing research, publications, and conferences about work teams. The site hosts TeamNet, a very active ListServe on team issues. (www.workteam.unt.edu.)

3M Meeting Network. This is a frequently updated site that provides lots of tips for improving the quality of meetings and facilitation. You will find information about meeting practices, tools, and services. You can sign up for the monthly 3M Meeting News. (www.3M.com/meetingnetwork/)

International Association of Facilitators. This is the web site for this small but important association of professionals who specialize in facilitation around the world. (www.iaf-world.org)

Zigon Performance Group. A leader in creating performance-measurement systems for work and teams. This site includes hundreds of performance measures and how-to articles on measurement systems. (www.zigonperf.com.)

Topical Index Of Activities

Note: A number of activities are found in several categories. These activities have multiple goals and can be used to achieve different outcomes.

	Page
Change	
24. Refreshing the Team	151
35. Teams That Change	225
Communication	
1. Bringing Up the Boss	11
4. Choice Role	25
15. How Do You Like to Receive Recognition?	93
27. Roadblocks	179
49. Wisdom	311
Conflict Resolution	
5. Communicating about Conflict	31
33. Team Conflict Mode	213

Consensus

27. Roadblocks   179
40. The Effective Team Member   243
46. Tough Jobs   295

Creativity

36. Tell-a-Story Teaming   227

Culture

 2. Building Trust among Team Members   13
13. Got Culture?   75
31. SOS   203
39. The Collaborative   239

Customer Relations or Satisfaction

 8. Customer Delight   47

Data-Collection Tools

 8. Customer Delight   47
13. Got Culture?   75
17. Improving Team Meetings   109
25. R E S P E C T   155
31. SOS   203
32. Team-Building Interview Guide   209

Decision-Making

22. Project Rescue   143
28. Selecting a Problem Solution   189
40. The Effective Team Member   243
41. The Product Development Team   253

42. The Quality Case   261
46. Tough Jobs   295
48. Virtual Consensus   309

Ethics

42. The Quality Case   261

Intergroup Team Building

9. Drawings   53
22. Project Rescue   143
29. Separate Tables   197
45. Tricky Tales   279
49. Wisdom   311

Leadership

1. Bringing Up the Boss   11
27. Roadblocks   179

Meeting Effectiveness

12. Freeze Frame   73
17. Improving Team Meetings   109
19. Meeting Monsters   121

Member Development

2. Building Trust among Team Members   13
4. Choice Role   25
5. Communicating about Conflict   31
15. How Do You Like to Receive Recognition?   93
20. My Team and Me   127
25. R E S P E C T   155
37. The Car Case   231

40. The Effective Team Member   243
44. TMS   273

Openers and Closers

6. Creating a Team Logo   37
10. E-Handles   55
11. Forming New Teams   59
18. It's a Puzzlement   113
21. Personal Ads   133
26. Rhyme Time   167
50. Yea, Team!   325

Organizational Assessments

31. SOS   203

Problem-Solving

22. Project Rescue   143
27. Roadblocks   179
28. Selecting a Problem Solution   189
37. The Car Case   231
47. Virtual Brainstorming   305

Recognition

15. How Do You Like to Receive Recognition?   93

Respect

25. R E S P E C T   155

Role Clarification

4. Choice Role   25
23. Really . . . but I Thought   149
44. TMS   273

Team Assessments

  3. Characteristics of an Effective Work Team   17
13. Got Culture?   75
17. Improving Team Meetings   109
20. My Team and Me   127
25. R E S P E C T   155
30. Skills for Sale   201
34. Team Development   219

Virtual Teams

47. Virtual Brainstorming   305
48. Virtual Consensus   309

Vision, Mission, and Goals

  7. Creating a Team Mission   39
14. Get Smart   85
16. How's Your Team's Vision?   101
20. My Team and Me   127
43. The Way We Are, and Want to Be   267

Index

accommodate, 215, 217
action plan worksheet, 195
action planning guide, worksheet, 23
action plans, 105–108
activity
    follow-up, 7
    preparation for, 6–7
    process, 7
assessment of team effectiveness,
        17–21
avoid, 215, 217

behavior, impacting team
        effectiveness, 73–75
being present for others, 162
brainstorming, virtual, 305–308
business modeling, 105
business team, 5

car case, 231–234
change
    planning for, 225–226
    refreshing team, 151–154
civility, 162
closers see openers and closers
collaborate, 215, 217
collaboration, 239–241
    advantages and disadvantages,
        167–178
    among teams, 53–54
    competition vs., 279–294
    cross-group, 311–324

cross-team, 293
communication
    about conflict, 31–36
    of feedback, 25–30
    with new boss, 11–12
    of recognition, 93–100
compete, 215, 217
competition
    advantages and disadvantages,
        167–178
    vs. collaboration, 279–294
compromise, 215, 217
conflict mode, 213–217
conflict resolution, 197–200
    lecture notes, 35–36
confrontation of problem team
        members, 121–126
consensus-building, 243–252,
        295–304
    guidelines, 251
    virtual, 309–310
contingency planning, 105
creativity, 227–230
cross-team-building, 279–284
culture of team, 75–84
    and applied strategic planning,
        105
customer perceptions, 47–49,
        51–52

data collection
    to assess respect, 155–166

on customer perceptions, 47–52
Survey of Organizational Support,
        203–208
team building interview, 209–212
on team culture, 75–84
on team meetings, 109–112
debriefing, 7
decision-making, 143–148
    ethical, 261–266
    without meeting, 309–310
development stage for team,
        219–224
drawings, for team collaboration,
        53–54
duration of team, 5

e-handles, 55–58
e-mail
    brainstorming by, 305–308
    participative decision-making by,
        309–310
effectiveness of team
    assessment, 17–21
    characteristics, 19–21
    communicating about, 31–36
    consensus-building, 243–252
    problem behaviors, 73–75
    roadblocks, 179–188
empathy, 161, 162
empowering, 161
environmental monitoring, 105
ethical decision-making, 261–266

expectations, 15, 149–150
extrinsic rewards, 100

feedback, 253–260
    about team member's role, 25–30
focus group, 47–52
focus of team, assessment, 101–108
free-falling team, 235–238

games
    to demonstrate collaboration,
        311–324
    to teach team concepts, 167–178
gap analysis, 105
get-acquainted activity, 113–120
    for new teams, 59–72
Getting to Know You worksheet,
    65–66
goals, SMART protocol for
    preparing, 85–92

high performance, development in
    team members, 235–238

icebreaker
    for large group, 325–332
    personal ads as, 133–142
identification with team, 127–132
implementation, 105
innovation, 227–230
interdependence, 13–14, 239–242
International Association of
    Facilitators, 334
interview, for team building,
    209–212
intrinsic rewards, 100
introductions for new teams, 59–72

Kropp, Dick, 334

leadership
    new for team, 11–12
    roadblocks, 167–178
lecture notes
    conflict resolution style, 35–36
    consensus method, 303
    trust, 15–16
listening, 125
logo, creating for team, 37–38

maintenance roles, 275
management team, 5

mature team, closing activity, 55–58
meetings
    improving, 109–112
    problem members in, 121–126
membership of team, 5
    performance, 235–238
mission of team
    creating, 39–46, 105
    evaluating, 45–46
motivation, 93–100
multivoting guidelines, 83

natural work groups, 5
negotiations with problem team
    members, 125
new product/service teams, 5, 55–58
new team leader, 11–12
new teams, get-acquainted and
    introduction, 59–72
norms for team, 125

obstacles
    to progress, 151–154
    to team effectiveness, 179–188
openers and closers
    e-handles, 55–58
    new teams, 59–72
    personal ads, 133–142
    puzzle, 113–120
    rhyme time, 167–178
    team icebreaker, 325–332
    team logo creation, 37–38
openness, 201
organization, support for teamwork,
    203–208

Parker, Glenn, 334
participative decision-making,
    without meeting, 309–310
performance audits, 105, 235–238
performance of team members,
    235–238
personal action plans, 235–238
personal ads, as icebreaker, 133–142
planning
    icebreaker, 225–226
    to plan, 105
    for team improvement, 17–24
positive reinforcement, 125
practice session, 7
predictability, 15, 16
prioritizing list items, 83

problem definition, 231–234
problem members, on teams,
    121–126
problem solving, 143–148, 189–196
    by geographically dispersed team,
        305–308
    skills, 13–14
problem-solving team, 5
product development team,
    simulation, 253–260
productivity, 227–230
progress, obstacles to, 151–154
project rescue, 143–148
purpose of team, types, 5
puzzle, for getting acquainted
    activity, 113–120

recognition, 151–154
    self-assessment, 93–100
respect, 155–166
    feedback survey, 165–166
rewards, 93–100
rhyme time, 167–178
roadblocks, 179–188
role clarification, 25–30, 149–150,
    273–278

self-assessment
    recognition, 93–100
    respect, 156, 159–166
self-direction, 223
self-oriented roles, 278
self-renewal, 224
simulation, product development
    team, 253–260
skills review, 201–202
SMART protocol, 85–92
strategic planning process
    first stages, 101–108
    worksheet, 105
survey
    of organizational supports,
        205–206
    of team culture, 77–82

task-oriented roles, 275
Task-oriented roles, Maintenance-
    oriented roles, Self-oriented
    roles questionnaire, 275
team building, 6
    cross-, 279–284

icebreaker, 325–332
interview guide, 209–212
team development grid, 219–224
Team Identification Model, 129–132
team logo, creating, 37–38
team meetings, improving, 109–112
team members, performance of, 235–238
teams
  assessment of status, 151–154
  closing activity for mature, 55–58
  collaboration among, 53–54
  culture, 75–84
  customer perceptions, 47–52
  observing dynamics, 243–252
  problem members, 121–126

stage of development, 219–224
strengths and weaknesses, 201–202
what they are, 4
teamwork, organization support for, 203–208
Tell-a-Story Teaming, 227–230
Things You Know You Know worksheet, 67–70
3M Meeting Network, 334
TMS questionnaire, 275
tough jobs, 295–304
training, 6
tricky tales, 279–294
trust, 13–16
  lecture notes, 15–16

University of North Texas, 334

values of team, 37–38, 105
valuing, 162
virtual brainstorming, 305–308
vision of team, 101–108, 267–272
  see also mission of team
visioning, 105

Web sites, 334
Wisdom (intergroup team game), 311–324
Workshops by Thiagi, 334

Zigon Performance Group, 334

About the Authors

Glenn Parker

Author and consultant Glenn Parker works with organizations to create and sustain high-performing teams, effective team players, and team-based systems. His best-selling book *Team Players and Teamwork* (Jossey-Bass, 1990) was selected as one of the ten best business books of 1990. Now in its seventh printing, *Team Players and Teamwork* has been published in several other languages and has been brought to the screen in an exciting new video entitled *Team Building: What Makes a Good Team Player?* (CRM Films, 1995). His training and team-building instruments, the *Parker Team Player Survey* (Xicom, 1991) and the *Team Development Survey* (Xicom, 1992), have become standards in the field.

Glenn is coauthor of *50 Activities for Team Building,* v. 1 (HRD Press, 1991), which was selected by *Human Resource Executive* as one of 1992's Top Ten Training Tools. He is the author of three resources for cross-functional teams: the book *Cross-Functional Teams: Working with Allies, Enemies and Other Strangers* (Jossey-Bass, 1994), a selection of The Executive Program Book Club and Soundview Executive Book Summaries, which was described as "a must for anyone charged with managing the future of the business"; the *Cross-Functional Team Toolkit* (Pfeiffer, 1997), a new manual; and *Cross-Functional Teams: The Simulation Game* (Xicom, 1998), which he codeveloped. Glenn is coauthor of *50 Activities for Self-Directed Teams* (HRD Press, 1994) and author of a collection of training resources and job aids entitled *The Team Kit* (HRD Press, 1995). He is also editor of the HRD Press *Best Practices for Teams,* volumes one (1996) and two (1998). His latest publications are *25 Instruments for Team Building* (HRD Press, 1998); *Teamwork: 20 Steps for Building Powerful Teams* (Successories, 1998); *Teamwork and Teamplay: Games and Activities for Training and Building Teams* (Pfeiffer, 1999); and *Rewarding Teams: Lessons from the Trenches* (Jossey-Bass, 2000).

Glenn does not just write about teamwork. He is a hands-on consultant and trainer who works with start-up and ongoing teams of all types in a variety of industries. He facilitates team building, conducts training workshops, consults with management, and gives presentations for organizations. His clients have included pharmaceutical companies, such as Merck and Company, Johnson & Johnson, Bristol-Myers Squibb, Hoffmann-La Roche, Rhône-Poulenc Rorer, Novo Nordisk, and Ciba-Geigy; a variety of industrial organizations, such as 3M, Kimberly-Clark, The Budd Company, Penntech Papers, Allied Signal, Pratt & Whitney, LEGO, BOC

Gases, and Bellcore and Siemens/ROLM Communications; service businesses such as Commerce Clearing House's Legal Information Service, Asea Brown Boveri (ABB) Environmental Services, American Express, Promus Hotel Corporation (Embassy Suites, Hampton Inns), and the *New England Journal of Medicine;* the sales and marketing organizations of Roche Laboratories and Pontiac Division of General Motors; health-care providers such as Aurora Health Center, Pocono Medical Center, St. Ann Taylor; and government agencies such as the Department of the Navy, Environmental Protection Agency, and National Institutes of Health.

Glenn holds a B.A. from City College of New York and an M.A. from the University of Illinois and has done doctoral work at Cornell University. He is a frequent speaker at corporate meetings and at national conferences sponsored by the American Society for Training and Development (ASTD), Lakewood Conferences, and the Center for the Study of Work Teams. He keynoted the BEST OF TEAMS '98 Conference. He is past president of the ASTD Mid-New Jersey Chapter and currently chairs the ASTD Publishing Review Committee.

Glenn is the father of three grown children and currently lives in central New Jersey with his wife, Judy. In his spare time he rides his bike, volunteers with the American Cancer Society, roots for the Philadelphia 76ers, and plans his next vacation.

Richard P. Kropp

Dick Kropp has successfully bridged the gap between the academic and business worlds. He has over 20 years of experience as an internal HRD consultant with such companies as General Motors, AT&T, First National Bank of Boston, and Wang Laboratories. At Wang, Dick was Director of Human Resources for Worldwide Operations, responsible for executive, management, professional, and technical employee development as well as all general Human Resource Management functions. He developed many innovative programs that were later adopted by other organizations.

He is currently the Managing Partner of The Kropp Group, Inc., a strategic and tactical consulting firm that specializes in Human Resource Management Systems, Corporate Education, and Instructional Design. The firm has content specialization in the areas of sales, sales management, customer service, and leadership and has worked with clients in the automotive, health-care, finance, sales, high-tech, research and development, and educational fields.

He serves as associate clinical professor in the Department of Education at Boston University, where he teaches graduate courses and assumes major responsibility for an innovative Master's Program in Human Resource Education. He holds a B.A. in theater from Mansfield University, an M.A. in communication from Temple University, and an Ed.D. from Boston University in human resource education, and has taught at Suffolk University and the University of Massachusetts.

He is an active member of the American Society for Training and Development (ASTD), and is past president of the ASTD Massachusetts Chapter and a former director of Region 1. He is also an active member of the HRD Professors Network and the HRD Consultants Network (where he served as national chairperson). He has been a speaker at several past ASTD national conferences, Region 1 conferences, and local chapter meetings.

He is coauthor of *Communicating in the Business Environment* (HRD Press, 1990), *50 Activities for Team Building,* volume one (HRD Press, 1991), and *50 Activities for Self-Directed Teams* (HRD Press, 1994). *50 Activities for Team Building* was selected as one of 1992's Top Ten Training Tools by the journal *Human Resource Executive.* He is currently working on two projects: a book on collaborative work structures and a series on business ethics and character in the organization.

In his spare time Dick enjoys golf, skiing, fine wine, and singing Irish folk songs.